Letting Go

The story of one man's journey
to live by faith and follow God

by

Todd Clevenger

with S.A. Kent

ISBN: 13: 978-1479398553

Barnabas Charities is a registered 501C-3 tax exempt organization. Your donation is 100% tax deductible and 100% of the profits from sale of this book go to Barnabas Charities. To donate, go to the website below and click on the donations tab or contact us at:

Barnabas Charities, Inc.
Fed ID #30-0215997
www.barnabascharities.org
www.facebook.com/barnabascharities
www.twitter.com/barnabascharity
Phone: 248-505-5554
E-mail: todd@barnabascharities.org

This book is available at barnabascharities.org.
Also at amazon.com and its worldwide distributors,
Including Kindle.
Retail stores can order through major book wholesalers

Cover design by Ben Schaal
Text editing, design and publication arrangements
by Sara Leeland Books
www.saraleelandbooks.net

Acknowledgements

I could not have completed this book without the many people who have made contributions of time, expertise, and support.

This book took over 1 1/2 years from the initial steps of interviewing to the gathering of information to writing and editing the book. What started off as a project to document my life has turned into a book about my spiritual journey that I hope will be an encouragement to others who read it.

As the book started to take shape, it was apparent that my message would resonate with others who have wanted to take a risk and follow an urge, but have resisted for many reasons. My experience is that the larger the risk, the larger the reward.

I would like to thank Sharon A. Kent who helped me write this book. Sharon believed in my story and thought this could have an impact on others. She has great talent and brought tremendous insight into this whole process.

I would like to thank the many people who were interviewed for this book. They all have special places in my heart as we have many experiences together. Some of them have supported me through difficult times while many others have provided me with spiritual advice and encouragement. They are: Anthony Paige, Pat Ball, Diane & Mark Beede, Diane Berry, Jerry Carnill, Ron Cline, Alex Clevenger, Charles Clevenger, Beth & Marc Clevenger, Torry Clevenger, Barbara Chilla, Justin Culver, Claudia Gallardo, Katrina Golden, Carol Holcombe, Steve Homich, Debbie & Eric McGough, Jean Richters, Pierre Roux, Larry Rubel, Lisa

Schulist, Lin Syzmanski, Norma Van Oss, Michelle Weed, and Peg & Tom Woodside.

Finally, I would like to thank others who helped in various ways. Sonwabo Jacobs, Stacey Singer-Leshinsky, and Kevin Syzmanski all provided me with inspiration without even knowing it. Ben Schaal of Iverdesign helped with technical and design work. Sara Leeland of Sara Leeland Books did the final edit and helped to publish the book.

Todd Clevenger
November, 2012

Dedication

This book is dedicated to my children
Alex and Torry.
You exemplify who Jesus wants us to be.
You both have such wonderful hearts
and truly care about other people.
I am so proud of how you have grown
into thriving young adults.
I love you both with all my heart!

A Barnabas Charities project providing
hand-woven hats to children
In third-world countries

Table of Contents

"Faith is a tall, tall order
and it's worth every terrifying moment
to never stop letting go."

–Todd Clevenger

Quito, Ecuador

I loved being a part of the team. I loved the country, the people, and especially the children. What I didn't love was seeing the conditions they all lived in. Their homes were inconceivably small by our standards in the United States. With less than 50 square feet in total interior space, it was nearly impossible for an entire family to lie down inside for shelter at night.

I saw children taking care of children. Many were street children, orphans or children who ran away from their homes to avoid abuse.

While trying to take it all in, I noticed a simple characteristic that made my heart ache. It was the children's hands. Starting with babies as young as two and three years old, their tiny hands were stained dark brown from picking through the garbage every day. Even though I knew we were going to Ecuador to serve the huge community living in the city dumps, I wasn't prepared for this reality.

Garbage trucks would arrive full of refuse and as the trucks dumped their loads, people were waiting to pick through the garbage to find what they could use to clothe themselves, build shelters, and if they were lucky, find something they could sell. I saw mothers picking through the rubbish with a baby in tow. As it all started to sink in I noticed that many children didn't have adequate shoes to protect their feet. In a third-world country where an infected cut can be fatal, being barefoot in a city dump is a huge problem.

Our group's destination was Quito, the capital city of Ecuador, which sits at the heart of the equator about 9,300 feet above sea level. The "middle of the world," as it's called by locals, is located in the Andes Mountains with one part of the city extending within a mile of Zero Latitude. As with most large cities, there are areas of extreme wealth and extreme poverty; we had arrived at the latter.

Some of life's most significant moments begin with an insignificant event. I was invited to a casual dinner one night in 2002 by good friends of mine, Tom and Peg Woodside. Before the evening ended I had agreed to go on a mission trip to Ecuador. The trip was sponsored by a humanitarian organization called Extreme Response; our mission was to host an annual event called the Christmas Party in the Dump.

These shacks are home to people who live in the dump.

The Woodsides had led teams on this trip several times before and, while it may sound a little Marie Antionette-ish to hold a Christmas party in a place where the need is so great, it is really an authentic way to show the love of Jesus through actions, not words.

When we first arrived at the dump in December, I was blown away by seeing a line a half mile long with what had to be 1,000 people, all waiting for the Christmas party to begin. All day long we celebrated through song, laughter and by presenting each child, many of whom had never received a gift before, with a wrapped Christmas present. I was humbled by the look on their faces as they received the small gift and realized that somewhere along the line these kids were taught to be thankful because every single one of them said, "thank you."

I couldn't help being in awe and I wanted to thank *them* for the gift of inspiration I was receiving. It also occurred to me that many kids in the United States would have tossed aside the little trinket as they moved on to their next Christmas present. I felt a little ashamed as I thought, "Wow! We could learn a lot from these people."

It wasn't unusual for one of the children to ask why we were there giving them presents. This question gave the team an opportunity to tell the Story of Christmas. We simply explained, "We gave you a present just like God gave the world Jesus because we love you as Jesus loves all of us." For some, it was the first time ever hearing someone tell them they were loved.

We prayed, but we didn't preach because little kids celebrating Christmas and playing with their gifts didn't want to hear about salvation or eternity at that moment; they just wanted to celebrate. The experience opened my eyes and I understood, maybe for the first time, what it meant to put faith into action. It was an ah-ha moment for me.

Later in the day, I was playing with a group of kids (I've been accused of being a big kid many times) and started a game of kick the can. It ended up being a haphazard game of soccer where two teams could only use their feet to move the can down the "field" and kick it between goals we made out of junk. As we were playing I started to think, "How can we get these kids toys, soccer balls, school supplies, and shoes for their feet?" Being in this beautiful country and meeting its people put a lot of things in my life into perspective. I've always heard people say how "mission trips will change your life," but I didn't get it until that day.

I couldn't stand feeling helpless, so my mind kicked into overdrive and I began my journey to make a difference in these kid's lives. Jerry Carnill, the founder of Extreme Response, probably said it the best when he told me, "Caring for the poor and putting your faith into action is about letting people see Jesus through what you do; not necessarily what you say."

The next day's events brought about a defining moment in my life, but what I didn't know was that more than a year would pass before the lesson would be revealed to me

Todd with a group of Ecuadorian children

Capturing an Image of Love

It was already raining as we drove up the barren land on the side of the Andes Mountains on route to a small hillside church where we would be attending a Sunday service. Only seven or eight miles outside the city of Quito, the differences between the city and this place were so great it could have been another world.

As we got closer I could see that the church was only partially sheltered and I knew we were in for a soggy day.

Congregation gathered in church to celebrate Christmas
(Note open walls at back)

Despite the weather, we had brought along Polaroid cameras to take pictures of the children and their families. In the United States, we are used to taking pictures of everything and anything. But in poor countries, cameras are not seen frequently outside the city. Many people did not have birth certificates or photographs to serve as a record of their children's lives. It affected me when I realized how important this picture might be to a child who had lost their parents. It may be the only record they have of their family. I learned that one of the ways we show Jesus' love in a third world country is by taking these family photographs.

Someone gave me a camera and that was it! I got so caught up in taking pictures that Tom and Peg, who were supposed to be taking pictures as well, gave up. Tom started feeding me film while Peg rounded up the families and got them lined up for a photograph. I managed to work around the language barrier because we enlisted local children to get family groups together.

We laughed and we gave thanks to God for the day and the hospitality of the people. I'm not sure how we pulled it all off in the rain and wind, but we did. Peg still teases me to this day saying, "We took a thousand images that day and learned that, if you're going to cut Todd loose with the camera, you better have a lot of film!"

My enthusiasm was the result of seeing the joy and surprised delight when children looked at the image of themselves and their family. With a humbled, full heart I realized we didn't just take pictures that day; we captured images of love.

"God, I'll Make You a Deal..."

I was tossing and turning, not able to sleep and eventually I gave up trying. That was when I decided to make a deal with God. I said, "Okay God, I know everything that is going on in my company and how much money we need. If I make $25,000 in profits this year, I'll donate the $4,500 to enclose the church." It seemed like a good idea at the time; a win-win situation for my company and the church. If you're already rolling your eyes and thinking, "Yeah, how'd that work out for you?"-- you won't be disappointed.

Part of my mistake was telling God what I thought was a fair exchange instead of praying for God to show me what He wanted me to do (the other part was making a deal in the first place). Clearly, I had the order of our relationship mixed up because I was still falling back into my habit of trying to be in control instead of following His lead.

Earlier that day, after we had finished the photo op and were making our way into the church for the Sunday service, I was amazed by the faith of the people in Quito. It had been rainy all day, but started raining buckets and the wind kicked up significantly. It was blowing so hard that it was literally raining into the church on one side. The people standing on that side of the church were drenching wet and had to be freezing, but they didn't seem to care. So I sure wasn't going to complain. They stayed to worship in spite of the adverse conditions and I remember thinking, "People probably wouldn't stick around to attend a church service in our country under these conditions." What a shame, too, because it was one of the most joyous and powerful services I've ever attended. God was definitely in the house.

In contrast to the world-renowned cathedrals of Quito, this small church was built into the side of the mountain and was not much more than a shell. It had a roof, but no walls and no doors to protect the few things the church owned. And as we experienced that day, there was little to offer protection from the elements to the congregation.

After the service, I spoke with the pastor, Remondo, who explained to me that they had a full church every week, rain or shine. But the people didn't have money, so constructing outer walls wasn't something they could do on their own. I was curious, so I asked Remondo what it would take to enclose the building. He said it would cost $4,500 American dollars. We talked for awhile longer about possible fundraising efforts to raise the money, but I didn't want to make any sort of commitment before giving it some serious thought.

Later that night as I struggled to fall asleep I made the "deal" with God to give Remondo $4,500 American dollars to enclose the church if my company made $25,000 in profits that year.

Feeling good about my promised philanthropy, I worked my tail off for the remainder of the year to hold up my end of the deal. The year ended, and after we finished the books in mid-January, I was disappointed to find that we only made $16,000 in profits. It was $9,000 less than what I needed in order to help the little Ecuadorian church. Still delusional, I thought, "Okay, I worked my end of the deal, but God didn't meet His end of the deal, so I don't have to pay the $4,500." I reasoned that it must not have been God's will and I was off the hook.

Days went by and instead of feeling relieved I couldn't shake the nagging heaviness in my heart. I talked about it with Tom and Peg Woodside and finally gave in and did what I knew was right. Although my company would be a little strapped, I knew donating the money was something I had to do. He was overwhelmed with surprised joy when the $4,500 in American currency was given to him. Evidently a lot of well-meaning people had made promises to Remondo in the past that were not kept. I wish I could have been there to see the celebration that ensued, but I didn't have to be there to feel their joy because it was mine as well.

The very next year my company, GB Synergy, made over $600,000 in profits! The strange part was that the more money I made, the more my heart was challenged to give. I've heard people say, "God is working in my life" and I was always happy for the person and sincerely meant it when I said, "Man, that's awesome!" But inside I really hadn't understood what they meant or were feeling. Now I did. When the purpose for being put on this earth was revealed by the Holy Spirit, I felt *free* and excited for whatever He had in store for me.

The deal with God didn't turn out as I thought it would, but I took a chance and listened to what the Father was telling me to do. Because of that obedience, I now had a purpose, a renewed passion and a hunger to not only improve lives, but to do it in the name of Jesus.

Barnabas Charities

After my firm's gift to the Ecuadorian church, Ideas were swimming around in my mind and a short time later I decided to start a Christian charity named "Barnabas Charities." The purpose of the charity was to help other people anonymously. We were able to keep that anonymity by giving gifts or money through Barnabas. I organized it as a 501C-3 non-profit organization and funded it by committing a percentage of profits from my company along with employee contributions.

It was such a great experience to witness the people I worked with opening their hearts and asking to get involved.

Tom Woodside used to kid me by telling people, "He already had a good heart, but this gave him something to do with his feet." It was true. I had the desire and drive to help people and starting Barnabas was like starting a business, only the goal wasn't to make money, it was to change lives.

I had taken the first step towards being involved in the missionary field. Working in missions on any level gives people the chance to step out of the church and do something more for God's Kingdom.

A lot of people think you have to be totally grounded and have the Bible memorized in order to be worthy of doing mission work. But that's not true at all. There are only a small percentage of people who actually preach; the vast majority of the people out there doing good work are volunteers and they are needed at all levels. There is also a tremendous need for practical knowledge like business, nursing, teaching and skilled trades of all kinds.

My eyes were opened to a whole new world of possibility where challenges were endless and there was truly an opportunity to make a difference in growing God's kingdom. I could begin to see His hand at work in my life through people that seemed to be strategically placed in my path to help me along the way.

One of these people was a friend and spiritual mentor, Jerry Carnill, who gave me confidence that I was on the right path. He opened my eyes to the fact that it doesn't take an extraordinary person to do this. It just requires someone who will step out of their comfort zone and take a chance. That is the extraordinary part.

I'd taken risks all my life in business and didn't think twice about putting it all on the line to start a new venture that I believed in. I began to see that I could do the same thing in ministry and be a part of changing people's lives by being someone God could use to help bring people to the place where their life can be changed. God does the changing, that's not my job, but I had heard God's calling and I was willing to take a chance by starting Barnabas.

Barnabas Charities was named after a character in the Bible by the same name. I felt an affinity with the man who was also called 'The Encourager'. Barnabas was a missionary who traveled with the Disciple Paul, preaching and spreading the word of God. He is first introduced in the Bible in Acts 4:36, *"Joseph, a Levite from Cyprus, whom the apostles called Barnabas (which means Son of Encouragement), sold a field he owned and brought the money and put it at the apostles feet."*

My greatest wish is to be a modern day Barnabas and encourage others to come to the Father. Patience is something I struggle with and I've had to learn to wait for God's timing. I have a tendency to try to help God in order to move things along at my speed, which doesn't always coincide with God's timetable. The obstacle I was repeatedly challenged to overcome was giving up control and letting God run the show.

(See end of book for more information on
Barnabas Charities)

Ready, Fire, Aim!

It was 8 p.m. on a September 2005 evening in Denver, Colorado, and we were on the road. As we pulled out of the subdivision, I remember Eric looking over at me with a look that said, "Oh man, what have I just gotten myself into!" He confirmed his sudden anxiety a second later as he asked, "You don't have a plan, do you?" I smiled and said, "Nope. But we'll figure it out as we go." That was probably the worst thing, that someone who likes things planned out in advance could have heard, but to his credit he never once backed down from the challenge. He was all in for whatever was to come.

Friends and neighbors had come by in droves to drop off cash and supplies to take with us, but Eric still had no idea that the mission was about more than just bringing supplies and helping out wherever we could for the three days we planned to be in Louisiana.

It was the infamous morning of Monday, August 29, 2005 when Hurricane Katrina smashed into Louisiana with such incredible force that it wiped out a quarter million homes and businesses, causing nearly 2,000 deaths and a dizzying $110 billion in damages to New Orleans and surrounding parishes.[1] The suffering was cycling on CNN 24 hours a day and I watched the news like a train wreck that I didn't want to see, but couldn't pull myself away.

In New Orleans, basic needs such as safe drinking water, plumbing or electricity were no longer available. I felt helplessly horrified for the people who were stranded on rooftops or trees, unsure of whether they would be rescued before Katrina swept them away. And I heard all the heartbreaking stories like a woman who was floating lifelessly, still clutching the hand of her child who had drowned in the flood.

Americans everywhere were bombarded with these stories and images as the number of victims increased day by day.

Katrina damage at one home

On Saturday, September 3, 2005, days after Katrina made landfall, I was tossing and turning all night not quite awake, but not asleep either. When I finally woke up that morning I knew I needed to go to New Orleans. The original plan was to contact friends and get the word out that I was going to take supplies to New Orleans. But by the end of the day I wanted to find a way to help people who were stranded in Katrina's wake.

I didn't have a clue how it was going to play out but a huge blessing came my way when my neighbor and good friend, Eric McGough, agreed to take the trip with me. It was a total leap of faith for both of us, but just taking off on this trip was way out of his comfort zone. The decision to go to New Orleans happened after I called him and said, "Eric, I'm taking supplies to New Orleans so if you and Debbie want to donate anything just stop by before 8 o'clock tonight." Then I randomly asked, "Hey, do you want to come with me?" I was happily shocked when he agreed.

Sometime later Eric told me about the quick exchange he had with his wife, Debbie, before committing to the trip. Chuckling as he remembered that time, he told me, "You know I am a very busy guy and far from spontaneous. But, for the first time in memory, I really had nothing going on during the Labor Day weekend. So I looked at Debbie and she kind of shrugged her shoulders like, 'It's fine with me.' So I said, 'Sure.' I had no idea you were leaving in 45 minutes!"

Eric got his things together quickly and we hit the road just after 8 p.m. The air conditioning hadn't even cooled my SUV yet when I looked over at Eric and saw an expression on his face that clearly communicated, "What the heck have I gotten myself into?"

Without looking over at me, Eric confirmed that he had guessed correctly when he said "You don't have a plan, do you?" Now he *was* looking at me. I had to smile and admit, "Nope, no plan. But I have an idea." Smiling now and shaking his head, he knew it was a total leap of faith for both of us.

All through the day, I had been e-mailing or talking by phone to a few contacts in the New Orleans area. There was no way to know if the information I'd gathered before we left was really credible. And, even if my contacts were credible, there was only so much anyone could know, given the loss of electricity and phones in the areas hit by the hurricane.

Surfing the internet, I couldn't believe the number of websites that had popped up over the past few days to assist the growing number of evacuees filling up shelters. There were thousands of people who sincerely wanted to help and were willing to donate homes, apartments, and even rooms within their houses. The problem was that the websites didn't provide contact information for those in the shelters to connect the parties making offers of help.

We talked about finding a way to bring the volunteers and evacuees together, and match them up quickly because we only had three days in New Orleans. I don't know why I didn't think of it immediately, but when I punched in the most obvious website name for this disaster there it was—the website that brought the whole plan together.

A woman named Katrina Blankenship had set up a website (www.katrina.com) that gathered names and phone numbers of people who had room available for others as well as the contact information for those looking to get out of the shelters. She had intuitively collected the information for both parties. The work just needed feet and that's where we would come in.

Everything started falling into place. The ride down was all business as we found connections all over the country. Neither of us slept. We were psyched to get busy and move people out of shelters and into homes.

Beyond Alexandria, Louisiana, there were no phone lines, electricity or gas stations in operation. So when a pastor we were in contact with also suggested Alexandria as a stopping point, we felt it was the right destination. Coincidently, my son's name is Alexander so I thought that was kind of a cool connection; maybe even a sign that this was where we were supposed to be.

Once during the ride we considered stopping in a different town until I called the pastor again to ask what he thought of the alternate destination. Apparently it wasn't my best idea because the pastor said, "Did I hear you are driving a Lincoln Navigator? You can't go there. Y'all will get carjacked and they'll shoot you!" Eric looked over and asked me, "You got a gun?" I said, "Nope, I'm not packin'."

So we stuck with Alexandria.

With that decision in place, I called a national hotel chain and was surprised to learn that there were hundreds of people taking shelter in those hotels. I explained to the manager what we planned to accomplish and he welcomed us to stay and set up in the lobby. He agreed to print out the massive list from Katrina.com and have a phone and working space set up by the time we arrived.

We had driven 17 hours straight through from Denver and were exhausted. Walking into the lobby I saw people everywhere; the lobby, the ballrooms and almost everyone was sleeping on the floor. When I walked up to the counter to check in, the clerk said there were absolutely no rooms available in the hotel.

At that point I didn't care. We would sleep in my SUV because neither of us would be able to get any rest in one of the chairs in the bright lobby. As it turned out, there was a lot of work for us to do because none of the promised preparations were done. There was no list, no phone and no work space. Eventually, the manager did give us a table and a couple of chairs to set up in the lobby and we also got the hotel to print the contact information for us.

Around 1 a.m., the night manager asked if we had found a place to stay and I said, "No." A room was suddenly available for us to stay in. It was crazy that with all these people sleeping on the floors, they had an empty room. Apparently, 'not available' did not mean the same as 'unoccupied'. After no sleep the night before, we were exhausted, so we took the room.

After Katrina hit, many places became shelters. Here's how it worked: A hotel would make itself available to be used as a shelter. The Red Cross was responsible for providing supplies like blankets for the Katrina victims who were staying in the hotel's convention rooms. The government paid the shelters a sum of money per/person, per/day as compensation for allowing the evacuees to stay. Some of the shelters did capitalize on the disaster, but many more had staff people who pulled out all the stops to help the evacuees.

We couldn't have been successful on our trip without a few of these key people.

One was a powerhouse of energy named Katrina Golden. This lady had a spunky, tell-it-like-it-is personality and a big heart to match. The ironic thing was that I never knew until years later that Katrina Blankenship and Katrina Golden were two different women. It turned out that my only interaction with Katrina Blankenship was through her brilliant website, but Katrina Golden and I became friends and worked together on a future trip to New Orleans 8th Ward.

Probably the most influential person I had the honor of working with during this trip was Doug Sterner. He connected me with people who put planes and a fleet of buses at our disposal to help with the logistics of what we considered our mission. Within 48 hours, an incredible team began working together to find homes--not simply shelter--for Katrina survivors.

Eric and I were in search of families needing help, while Doug worked with Retired Special Forces Captain Robert Noe and his wife Kathy, who lived in Alexandria. It was crazy how Alexandria kept coming into the picture. Clearly, we had not headed there by coincidence.

Joining the team was student pilot Cullen Canazares and his wife Christina, who began arranging flights from shelters in Louisiana and Texas to homes around the country. The incredible people Doug put me in contact with allowed us to get anyone from one place in the country to another with one phone call.

A little more background about Doug Sterner. If you met him for the first time, you'd find him a good natured, salt-of-the-earth kind of guy with a love of family and country. What you would discover as you came to know him better is that Doug served in two tours of the Vietnam War, is an author of over 100 books, a historian, and considered to be the foremost authority in the nation on America's highest award for valour, the Medal of Honor.[2]

His website, www.homeofheros.com, receives about 15 million hits each month. It has been featured on *Fox News*, in the *New York Times, Reader's Digest, The Chicago Herald, Focus on the Family* radio broadcasts*, and on CNN.*[3] I was in awe of how God was putting people in my path to make this effort work.

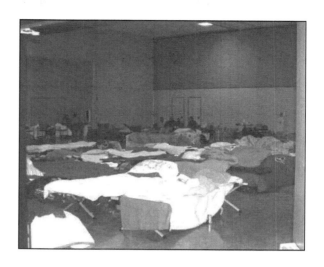

One evacuee shelter in
Alexandria, LA.

After closing our eyes for a couple of hours, but not really sleeping, we set up at the table in the lobby with a pot of coffee and started working with the contact list from katrina.com that the hotel clerk had printed for us overnight.

Eric and I had geared up for this moment since leaving Denver and were ready to start making things happen for the people in the shelter. I've never been shy about talking to strangers and usually they are comfortable with me as well, but this time, my enthusiasm was met with skeptical resistance.

It took a few seconds to regroup and try to put myself in their shoes. I realized they had no idea what our intentions were. They just lived through a horrific event in their lives, leaving them homeless and feeling more than a little vulnerable. So I changed tactics and approached them by introducing myself and simply asking how I could help.

A favorite quote of mine is from Mother Teresa, who said: "Never worry about numbers. Help one person at a time, and always start with the person nearest you."

This was the approach we took. At first, people were distrustful. A few asked, "Are you guys with FEMA?" I wasn't sure if answering "yes" would have been a good thing or a bad thing; but I said, "No, we're not with FEMA. We're just two guys from Denver who want to help. We have resources to get you relocated to friends, relatives, or to match you up with people who have made housing available."

As we helped people, word spread in the hotel and it didn't take long before we were really in business. Then I asked, "Do you have family somewhere? Is there somewhere you want to go?" Our plan worked like this: I'd ask where the person wanted to go. If they had family they wanted to stay with, then I'd call and let the person speak with them directly.

It seems like a simple thing, but many people didn't have phones; so, even if there was someone they could stay with, they didn't have a way to communicate. Then the more difficult part was finding a way to get to their family. Just as many didn't have phones, they didn't have cars or money. It was a dire situation and we were so blessed to be able to help.

If they didn't have family or friends to stay with, I asked where they wanted to go, and then found someone on the list with housing available in that area. The next step was to call that person, introduce myself and give a brief spiel about how I got their contact information. Then I'd say something like, "You posted on the website that you have a house available for a Katrina victim. Is it still available?" If it was, I'd tell them: "I have a family here; 2 adults, three kids… and I think it would be a good match. Does that sound good?" If they agreed, the final step was to connect the two parties by asking, "Okay, can I put them on the phone so you can talk to each other?"

That last step was the most important. It was one thing to match them up, but we had unintentionally stumbled across the essential element—getting the two parties talking to each other. Once they talked, the anonymity was gone and it was two human beings; one in need and one who wanted to help. The key to making the list work was establishing that relationship.

A New Orleans couple who had lost family members

Once we had the green light to move forward, we had to arrange transportation to get the family to their destination. If they had a car, I gave them cash for gas and food. If they needed to fly or take a bus, then I'd arrange that through the contacts Doug Sterner provided. Whatever it took, that's what we did.

The flood gates opened and we were able to start putting our resources to work, relocating family after family after family. Eric and I were completely in synch as a team and within 24 hours we relocated over 100 families! No business venture had ever given me such a feeling of success or purpose. I experienced firsthand that 'God has it covered'. It showed me that we need to trust Him and follow Him because, if we're doing God's will then we cannot fail, period.

The reason we were in Alexandria was to help people get out of the shelters, but somewhere along the way it expanded to see if there was anyone who wanted to caravan back to Colorado. Next thing we knew, the project had ballooned into a convoy of eleven families travelling back with us to La Junta, Pueblo and Denver.

Alexandria, **top left; New Orleans, bottom right**

From lower right: La Junta, up to Pueblo,
Colorado Springs, and Denver—
cities where refugees would find new homes

Convoy

Before leaving Alexandria, a friend from Denver called me saying, "Hey, you were on TV!" I laughed. And, thinking there must be a punch line coming, told him, "Not likely. I'm down here in Alexandria." Then he shocked me saying, "Dude, you were just on Larry King Live! Barbara Bush just told your story on Larry King Live!"

It turned out that the President and First Lady Bush were being interviewed together about Katrina on Larry King Live.[4] She didn't say my name, but the First Lady did talk about what we were doing. I was floored that our little grass roots effort was receiving national attention. I also suspected that Doug Sterner had something to do with the First Lady hearing about our efforts.

Newspapers and television news were now calling, trying to get interviews. There was so much sadness over the personal tragedy associated with the hurricane that the nation really wanted to grab on to stories of hope. I couldn't justify talking to the press and missing the opportunity to get a family relocated. I was happy for the publicity because it spread awareness and hopefully spurred other people into action who wanted to help but didn't know how to go about it. I was frustrated because I didn't know what to say. I couldn't tell an evacuee, "Hey, can you wait a minute to be relocated while I talk to CNN or Fox News?"

As we worked in Louisiana, back home in Denver our wives were spearheading an effort to locate families who were willing to open their houses or donate rental homes. Debbie McGough, Eric's wife, took on the role of organizing donations, which was getting to be a huge effort because of the growing media coverage. There were people coming out of the woodwork asking how they could contribute.

It was a huge outpouring of compassion, with donations from the citizens and businesses in Denver that included dozens of gift cards from Kings, Target, and Safeway, along with furniture, clothing, and much needed winter coats, mittens and boots for the families when they arrived. The evacuees were from the Deep South where few if any had ever seen snow, much less experienced a Colorado winter.

Then our time was up and it was time to get moving.

The group who caravanned back to Colorado with us

It was a four-day holiday because of Labor Day, but today was Monday and Eric needed to be back in his office on Tuesday. We gathered close to 30 people (and a couple of dogs) that wanted to relocate to Colorado. The stress level was high because the people were leaving their lives behind to move to Colorado on faith. It didn't occur to me until after we were committed what a tremendous responsibility this trip put on my shoulders, but I wasn't going to let them down.

Our convoy was made up of seven cars and my SUV. Some of the cars were in rough shape, but they were packed up with all of their owner's possessions and we were ready to roll. Most were leaving all they ever knew and trusting that we were bringing them somewhere they could make a new home.

The three towns—La Junta, Pueblo and Denver—got behind our grass roots effort. Houses full of furniture were being readied for their new residents, some job opportunities had been lined up, and full scale celebrations were planned by the generous people in these three cities. They were complete with news crews, balloons, a banquet of food, and hundreds of people giving a hero's welcome to the people from New Orleans.

I had the timing of the trip all planned out. There were people waiting to greet the newcomers in each of the cities so I had to give them an idea when we would arrive. I made sure to cushion the timetable for getting gas, food, and bathroom breaks. I also felt a sudden anxiety as the responsibility of leading the convoy back to Colorado hit home and I realized that this journey might be much more stressful that I had envisioned.

There were logistics to consider. We had eight vehicles with people who were literally counting on us for everything. It dawned on me how critical it was to keep the convoy together. If we lost one of the cars because someone fell behind, or their car broke down, or they just got separated from the convoy because of stoplights and traffic, it would be a very serious problem.

After being evacuated, people only had whatever money they'd brought from home, and most had never lived outside of Louisiana. The reality struck me that anyone in the car left behind would be stranded in a totally unfamiliar area without money for food or gas. To make matters worse, not every car had a cell phone which meant we couldn't communicate with everyone directly.

"Necessity is the mother of invention," as the Greek philosopher Plato said long ago. We developed a signal system for the convoy to communicate with each other. If someone needed to stop they would flash their headlights. The car in front of them would then do the same and so on until it got to my car. When I got the signal, I would pull over and the rest would follow suit. The system worked surprisingly well and we never lost anyone.

The need for bathroom breaks frequently caused the lights to start flashing. Each stop added time to the length of the trip and set back my timetable. I was getting frustrated because I am the type of person that prefers to drive straight through with as few stops as possible. Just think of a family car trip you've taken. If you're like most, you can recall Mom and Dad commenting on the 'needed' bathroom breaks 20 minutes after you had just stopped, because *someone* didn't go in to the bathroom. Multiply that by eight cars and you'll get a sense for what it was like.

I stayed focused on the end game and the group started referring to me as 'The General'.

Stops were as expensive as they were time-consuming. When we stopped to eat, Eric and I would give a $20 bill to each family as they went into McDonalds, Burger King, or wherever we stopped. Gas prices had risen to $4.50 per gallon in some areas, so when all 8 cars stopped for gas it could cost upwards of $600.

We did whatever we could in order to keep moving the group along, and, when my cash ran out, I started using credit cards. We tried to take care of everyone. I remember buying a couple of movies for the little kids to watch in the back of my vehicle. One little girl picked out *Legally Blonde* with Reese Witherspoon—a total chick flick. Their dad, a great big guy who was in the back seat with the kids, groaned when they put the movie in and said, "Man, take me back to the flood."

Eric had given up any hope of going to work on Tuesday, but I still wanted to drive straight through because people were waiting for us in all three towns. In the end, everyone was tired, so we stopped at a hotel for the night. I was elated when we checked in and the manager gave us the rooms for $15 each after hearing our story. The hotel staff was amazing; they took care of everyone which gave me a moment to breathe.

One of the men travelling with us, Ernest, was homeless before Katrina and was a seriously scary dude. When the rooms were handed out, Eric and I decided it would be best for us to room with him. We weren't totally comfortable about it because there was something about his stature and persona that was really intimidating.

Fortunately there was an extra room, so we let Ernest have it since he was travelling alone. But man, were we in for a surprise at the transformation from the time we met him until the time we arrived in Denver. By the end of the trip he had softened and opened up to us. Ernest hadn't experienced a lot of kindness in his life that didn't come with a price tag, so it took a while for him to let his guard down and believe that we were sincerely there to help with no hidden agenda.

This was the second time in three days where I saw kindness met with skepticism and outright distrust—and then transformed. It made me want to do more to help others. A Ruth Smeltzer quote says what we experienced: "You have not lived a perfect day, even though you have earned your pay, until you have done something for someone else who will never be able to repay you."[5]

Kindness without the expectation of getting any-thing in return is a gift we give to ourselves.

A Match to the Tinderbox

All of a sudden I saw headlights furiously flashing behind me and I knew in my gut something was seriously wrong. What I didn't know was people in some of the cars were getting text messages from friends and family saying that CNN just ran a story about a woman who was killed in a rescue attempt—and it was George's missing wife.

A meltdown had been simmering just below the surface as the stress of the journey increased proportionately to the awareness of what they had just done by leaving their homes and everyone they knew behind. Everyone was missing someone because families had been separated and they didn't know if their loved ones were dead or alive. Some of the travelers didn't have licenses and I even suspected that one of the cars may have been stolen. To top it all off, no one had slept well the night before. In retrospect it was just a matter of time before someone lost it. The text messages lit the fuse.

George was a passenger in the car when the text came through. Chaos exploded when the news story went on to report that the children, George's children, were in a shelter. CNN didn't report where George's kids were, so they had no idea what town his kids were in. George was devastated when he learned his wife died, but he was inconsolable when he thought of his children being in a shelter among strangers after just losing their mother. He didn't know if his kids had witnessed her death, but the possibility was all too real. It was unspoken, but as loud as if shouted that his kids were alone and probably terrified. As a parent, I know there is no greater fear than having our children be in jeopardy and not being able to protect them.

That was all it took; the group was already a tinderbox of suppressed emotion, and the news spread like a quick fire. It was in that moment that a dangerous situation suddenly developed. Born of fear, frustration, panic, and utter devastation, George's pain became their own and it was unbearable because it was the news they all feared.

I typically perform best under pressure, but this was different. I felt responsible for these lives and in a second, the people I'd sworn to protect and find shelter for had just 'lost their minds'.

I look back and see that I should have been seeking God to be 'The General' instead of trying to bear the responsibility on my shoulders. Still, God was silently with me because, although the situation was terrifying, a sense of calm came over me as I went into damage control mode. It was like being in an accident where everything goes into slow motion and I felt intensely focused.

It was no longer a matter of just getting my crew to their destination. Now I had to keep them from harming themselves or others out of the sheer depth of their grief. It sounds melodramatic, but the emotion the group was experiencing was the culmination of the utter devastation they had just survived.

They had watched everything they owned be destroyed by Katrina. They had been corralled into a shelter where they had to sleep on floors with their families, or what they had left of their families. On top of it all, they were leaving the only place some had ever lived to follow a stranger to Colorado and start their lives over again. We may have compassion, but how can anyone who didn't live through it truly understand their despair?

I was aware of the very real possibility of one of their cars being involved in an accident and the accompanying risk of endangering their lives. Eric was my rock. The first thing we did was to pull over and stop the cars in the convoy.

Then we went from one car to the next, consoling them, talking to them and praying with them. George was in a car with four other guys who were trying unsuccessfully to comfort him. I looked at George while I told them with a confidence I didn't feel, that we just needed to get to the houses waiting for them. I asked them to trust me and keep going because we didn't even know if the text message about the story was true.

After a while the panic ebbed enough that I could get the group back on the road. I had no illusion about their precarious emotional state and I was thankful they were not on the side of the road any longer with cars whizzing by. Eric and I had both been praying that none of our people would get hit.

As soon as we got back on the road I started making phone calls to my contacts asking them to connect with CNN and Fox News to validate the story, and, if it was true, to find out where George's kids were. CNN and Fox News had been following our story for some time and they saw the potential for a great personal interest piece. Meanwhile, I was thankful that George was in a car with four other men to help keep his situation under control.

La Junta, Colorado, was our first destination. The town had a huge welcome celebration ready for the newcomers, with food and music and hundreds of people who came out to give them a warm and enthusiastic welcome. In addition to the celebration, they had duplexes set up, fully furnished, and even had clothes for the children and adults. Out of compassion and love, the community pulled together in a time of great need to make a difference in the lives of strangers.

But I still didn't feel comfortable about bringing the group into a full scale celebration in their current state of mind. I called La Junta's mayor and said, "Hey, we have a problem. I can't bring these people in to the city's welcoming crowd." I told the mayor about the CNN news story and the subsequent meltdown of the group. "You have to give us a back way to come in." He immediately understood and said, "No problem, just tell me what you need."

We were given an alternate route so we didn't have to go through the center of town, allowing us to arrive quietly. Two families would settle in La Junta, but I knew the entire group would be hungry, so I asked if they could have food ready for the group. The last favor I asked for was to have a mechanic take a look at one of the cars and let me know if it could make the trip to Pueblo. The car wasn't in the best shape when they left Louisiana and travelling 1300 miles had taken its toll.

The mayor took care of everything.

To our surprise and the group's delight there was a feast waiting for them. Eric and I had an understanding that one of us would be with them at all times after the recent incident. I couldn't eat, so Eric went in to thank everyone and watch over the group. I was still unnerved by what had happened earlier and not entirely convinced the trouble had passed. So, while the rest were eating, I went to talk to the mayor and told him that half of the group wanted to return to Louisiana to help locate George's kids. And I told him that I felt I couldn't let the group break up now when they were so close to making it to their destination.

The mayor seemed to understand where I was coming from and suggested we gather the group and talk to them as a whole. So I did. I let them know that I had people checking into the story with CNN and Fox News to find out if it was true, and if it was, to find out where George's kids were so that we could bring them together.

I was pretty sure they were thinking about their own loved ones and who was going to help them reunite, so I gave them the hard truth that, logistically, the authorities weren't letting anyone back into New Orleans. Even if that changed, there was still no electricity, food, gas stations or cell phone reception available there. I urged the group, with all the sincerity I could convey, to let us get them to the homes waiting for them, and to then take a breath before deciding what they each wanted to do. I hoped for clarity, but couldn't tell if I was truly getting through.

No sooner were we packed up and ready to get back on the road when one of the men from the group ran up to me and Eric shouting, "George just took off!"

"What do you mean, 'George took off'?" I asked as fear clutched my heart.

The man replied in a frantic tone, pointing in the direction of the highway saying, "George just took off on foot."

Eric could tell I was going after him and said, "Tell me what you want me to do." I took off running after George and yelled over my shoulder, "PRAY!"

I was acting on instinct and adrenaline; all I knew at that moment was I had to get to George. Simultaneously, Eric quickly assigned people to watch over the others as he called his wife Debbie and said, "We've got a problem. We need prayers...right now!" Then he gave her a quick run-down of what happened.

Debbie didn't waste any time; she called their pastor, Kevin, who reached out to others and before long calls for prayer were branching out in all directions. We learned some time later that there were people all over Colorado sending up prayers for us, including friends, family, church members, and even some members of the news crews who had set up camp so they could be there when the group arrived.

As I ran down the road, I spotted George about 100 yards ahead of me and I was shouting at the top of my voice for him to stop. I was spent when I finally caught up with him. George was crying incoherently, consumed with the agony of knowing his children were out there and needed him and he couldn't reconcile going to a safe place to live when they were out there alone and probably scared.

I was terrified he would do something crazy, so I literally ran into him with a tight hug partly to console him, but mostly to get him back from the road. George was not a small man so it took all of my remaining strength to hold him while try-ing to calm him down.

"What are you doing?" I asked.

George shook with angry tears and resolutely said, "I have to go back."

Keeping a hand on him to keep him from bolting again, I said, "What are you talking about? George, you can't walk 1,300 miles. You have to get a hold of yourself so we can figure this out!" I never took my hand off him the whole time. It was the only thing I could think of to steady and calm him. In a quiet voice I pleaded, "Please George, just come with us. You can't go back now because there's nothing to go back to. We'll find your kids, George. I promise we'll find them."

George was talking nonsense when he stopped mid-sentence, dropped his head and shook it slowly as if waging an internal battle. He let out an agonized moan and his posture slumped in a defeated pose as he admitted, "I was going to walk out in front of a truck."

Finally - that's what I knew to be true all along. I felt like I could breathe for the first time since hearing that he ran off. I hoped that because George admitted the truth out loud, he was out of immediate danger. It was the first understandable sentence out of his mouth in about five minutes. The words were frightening, but they were said in such a way that I felt he might be getting a grip on his emotions.

While we were sitting on the side of the road, I happened to look over my shoulder and see a group of rough guys who had obviously been drinking, or worse. Instantly I started praying because this was not the time to pick a fight with George. So I started to pray, "God, please protect George. Please, we've come this far..."

Literally a moment later one of the cars in our convoy drove up, and inside were the three other men who were travelling with George. All I could think was, "Thank you, God, for coming through!" The guys persuaded George to get in the car and waited expectantly for me to join them. When I didn't move Eric said, "Aren't you coming?"

I told them, "Go on ahead and I'll be there in a few minutes." I needed to walk and clear my head. It was a big deal because I was accountable for their safety and they were my responsibility.

I met the group back at the gathering in La Junta and was getting everyone together, when I noticed a car was missing. Not knowing that a mechanic had taken it back to his garage to fix it at no charge, I lost it and shouted, "Where is the car?" There may have been an unfortunate expletive in there somewhere, too. Then someone told me what had happened and I calmed down and asked that they just get the car back so we could leave for Pueblo.

After that happened, I sat on the curb and cried. It wasn't about the mechanic taking the car back to the garage to fix it, I just had enough. And to add insult to injury, I was embarrassed and ashamed that I had lost control in front of people who were doing their best to help. Not too long afterwards, the car was returned and the remaining group got back on the road.

When we arrived at Pueblo there was another huge welcome. Four families would be making this their new home. The spread of food in Pueblo was as great as it was in La Junta, and the group was definitely enjoying themselves again. Many people went up to the newcomers and shook their hands, congratulating them on having the courage and faith to make the trip. The four families staying in Pueblo were greeted, given immediate medical evaluations and after we left they were given rent-free/utilities-free homes that were also fully-furnished and stocked with food.

As before, I stayed in the background, but before we left I had the honor of meeting Doug Sterner, the founder of Home Of Heroes, face-to-face. He really is an extraordinary man. Doug gave me a medal that was minted by his organization to commemorate what he said was my service to our fellow citizens. I was glad it was just between us because I would have been uncomfortable if he had presented it to me in front of everyone. I didn't feel deserving, but I felt honored by Doug. It certainly feels good whenever you help people, but there are so many families and faces that you can't help. I couldn't help feeling there was more we could have done—there could always be more.

I was edgy and just wanted to get to Denver. Well-meaning people were constantly calling me to get an update on our status. I knew they had prepared a celebration in Denver, complete with news crews and a couple hundred people all waiting to greet us. So I told the group they had about 30 minutes. When that time was up, I announced, "Whoever is going on to Denver needs to make their way to the cars now. We are leaving in 5 minutes!"

Someone had contacted the local TV station and they wanted to broadcast our arrival live on the news. I was furiously trying to figure out how we could get from Pueblo to Denver on time. I didn't realize it, but Eric said, "Todd, you're driving 100 mph and we are losing everyone."

That was the moment that I realized I had again been trying to do it my way. The group was and had always been in God's care, not mine. Instead of having my timetable, I should have prayed for God to show me the way and let things play out in His time. I prayed right then and there. I gave up and let God handle it. I knew we were not going to make it to Denver in time to be on the news or for the celebration—and I was totally at peace with it. The stress lifted off my shoulders after finally surrendering the situation to God.

When we arrived in Denver, there were still around 50 to 100 people waiting to welcome us home. We didn't arrive in fanfare; the news and TV crews had long since left, but the people who meant the most were there.

Eric described the moment best:

> We planned all along to wrap the trip up at GB Synergy. When I walked into the foyer, everyone was clapping and I remember being shocked because it was late but there were all kinds of people there: people from my church, friends, colleagues from work, my wife, and my kids. It was very emotional and it was a huge relief to finally be home. It's so amazing the hand God had in our trip and in keeping us all safe.

I was just relieved to have made it home. The trip had taken its toll and I just wanted to go home, get into bed and sleep for a month. I told the group to go into the GB Synergy building, but I saw my wife and held back. I was emotionally spent. When my wife saw me, she stopped and said, "Wow, you look like you aged at least five years."

I remember saying, "It wasn't that I aged five years over the past several days, I aged five years over the past six hours!" Then she hugged me and we headed home.

The next day we received a miracle. The people from Fox News had tracked down the story and found George's kids, *and* their mother. His wife was not the woman who had passed away. She was alive and the children were with her, waiting to be reunited with their dad. The news was received with joy, but tempered with sadness because there was the unspoken knowledge that it was someone else's mother or daughter or wife that had died. Everyone with us had lost so much.

It was also a time of new beginnings. Living in Colorado couldn't erase what the Louisiana people had lost, but it did help with the healing process. Their new surroundings meant that they didn't have to wake up every morning to see the

Damien and Kim, a couple who lost everything in New Orleans, relocated to Denver with us and were married in my home.

destruction, quickly turning into the moldy decay of their former homes. It was a time to be thankful and begin to move forward. All I can say is "Thank God!" Thank you for bringing us all home.

Evidently, God's plan wasn't for us to arrive in fanfare. Maybe it wouldn't have been good for the people from New Orleans. I can honestly say I worked with the intention of doing God's will, but it seems I forget that God has it handled and wants obedience before action. Similar to the deal I made with God in Ecuador, I learned what I was supposed to do after the process was nearly over. Apparently I like learning lessons the hard way and as Shakespeare wrote in *Hamlet*, "Therein lies the rub." A disguised obstacle to really knowing the Lord is our desire to be in control over situations in our lives.

One step is simply acknowledging that we want God to be in control of our lives. Like many things, if we feel we "have" to do something, we naturally don't want to do it.

Of course the converse is also true, right? In my world, if someone says I "can't" do something, it goes right to the top of the list of things I want to do most. A powerful lesson came from pastor C. Troy Sibley from Slidell, Louisiana, who shared a new way of dealing with feelings of the flesh. He said, "Instead of fighting against our natural feelings, let whatever it may be flow right through you and then hand it over to Jesus because He will take the burden from you. Sometimes that means excusing yourself from the table and praying quietly alone, 'Jesus, I give these feelings of [name the feeling] to you' over and over. I promise God is good and He will handle it."

The lesson I took away from this experience was that while I had good intentions and followed God's call when He told me to go to Louisiana, I was too focused on the end-game to see that I needed Him to call the plays. In order to serve Christ, I learned that I have to take the "me" out of the equation completely. It's either all for God's glory, in God's timing, according to God's plan, or it's not. It is really that simple. And regardless of where we are in our walk, wanting to follow God but also wanting to be in control is the paradox all Christians will face.

An online publication, *Intervarsity*, beautifully illustrates the power and purpose of prayer in our journey to let go and let God lead us:

> Prayer is not a grocery list of wants or a way to change God's mind, but a way to regain per-spective in our relationship with God. We pray to remind ourselves of our place of humility, to re-

mind ourselves that God is God, and we are not. Submitting ourselves to God in prayer changes *us*. God loves us enough to transform us into all that He created us to be. But we must cooperate in that transformation; and every time we pray, we cooperate just a little bit more.[6]

And, as I was learning, it's a journey not a light switch.

Todd and Eric McGough

Justin and Ernest

Ernest was the "seriously scary" guy who came back to Denver with the convoy of people from Alexandria. He was paired with Justin Culver who was the young CEO of a Denver based IT company. Justin responded to the destruction and suffering caused by Katrina, but he wanted to do more than write a check. He was interested in opening his home to help out tangibly. He got what he asked for in a big way! This is a story of one of the 30 people who travelled from Louisiana to Colorado.

Justin told his story by giving a little laugh at the relative absurdity of how he came to be paired with Ernest, and how the experience challenged him, made him laugh, and enriched his life all at the same time.

I wanted to be a part of the help. I have a three-bedroom home and I had extra room, so I put it out there on the website and made my house available if someone needed a place to stay. Somehow, the information from the website was linked to Barnabas Charities and Todd.

I got a call from Todd saying he was going down to New Orleans and bringing refugees back. He said, "If you want to meet us at GB Synergy and take someone home then you can." So that's exactly how it happened. I showed up at Todd's offices when Todd and Eric rolled up with a car full of people and that's literally how Ernest came to stay with me for a couple of months.

I hadn't met Todd yet, so it was pretty intense. But that's how God works in my life. It's cool. I like to be stretched and throw myself out there. God always protects me and it was a unique opportunity. Taking Ernest in for a while was challenging, but the relationship that I've built with Todd since then has made every bit of stretching I went through during that time worth it.

It's how God works. You kind of have to step out a little bit and then you're like, "WOW!" I definitely felt a tug on my heart; there was no question. I knew the difference when I was sitting there reading the paper. I don't always just feel generous and want to bring a stranger into my home. So when God put it on my heart I thought, "Okay this is what God wants me to do and it's going to work out." When that happens, I have confidence about doing it.

Ernest was a guy they almost wanted to leave behind because he seemed dangerous. He was from the streets and just had a really intimidating presence. They originally matched Ernest up with a lady, then thought, "Nah, maybe that's not such a good idea. Maybe it would be a better idea for him to stay with Justin."

It was exactly what I'd hoped for. I really wanted to help someone out. I think coming to Denver was a better situation than what Ernest had in New Orleans. He had been living in the streets at the time; homeless. He had to sleep with the radio on. Not some soft rock station, it was the local Rap station (FM 1075); and it wasn't not just on, it was blaring!

Then he started testing the limits of what I would give him. He was apt to say, "Hey, could you give me some money? I need some to send back to [insert name] in New Orleans."

It was the street mentality of: I'm going to stay in this guy's house and I'm going to get whatever I can. I gave him a little bit at first, but I tried to be pretty smart about it because I wanted to be able to help in a tangible way, not enable him to take advantage of the situation.

He definitely kept in touch with me all throughout the day. He didn't have a car so he needed rides. Things like that are what I'd signed up for because I wanted to make a difference in his life by bringing him in and helping him get a new start in life. I'd go with him and wait in line to get a job. Then get him to and from his job. That turned out to be a challenge, so I got him a used car.

It was fun, too, and I think there was culture shock on both ends. One time I was having a Bible study with a bunch of Denver people. Ernest was there and wasn't shy about participating. We'd be discussing the subject when he would interject something and make us all laugh. I think it was good for all of us.

His family was still missing when he came to Denver, but it was a miracle when his wife and kids came back on Todd's second trip to New Orleans and he moved out shortly thereafter. His family was able to get housing from an organization in Denver. I kept in touch with him for a while until they moved to another city and then we lost contact.

A couple of years later, I was at the city park in downtown Denver, just playing my guitar, when a big black guy came up and said something to me like, "Hey! What's your problem man?"

I thought, "Oh no, I'm going to have to use my guitar as a weapon against this huge dude."

He said my name a couple of times before I recognized that the guy was Ernest! He was just messin' with me. This was in the summer of 2010 and I hadn't talked to him in two years. He had gained some weight and his hair was in really long braids. He seemed to be doing well and it was cool to see the way God worked his life out.

This experience helped to push me further in my own faith by getting to know Todd, his love for life and the crazy way he dreams. He says things like, "If we serve a God that created the universe, then why can't we [fill in the blank]?" And it would be something ridiculously ambitious. It's probably critical for what he wants to accomplish, for Todd – being as ancient as he is at 48—still has that love for life and is able to dream big.

Who is Todd?

I'm not an extraordinary guy. I was born in Holland, Michigan, home of the Tulip Festival. I was the youngest of three children and my siblings would say "the spoiled one who got away with everything." It's not true of course, but there you have it.

I remember my childhood being nearly idyllic. My parents, Norma and Chuck, owned and ran their own businesses, so I grew up in an environment that encouraged risk taking. I had my first paying job when I was about three years old, helping my dad put F.O.R.D. stickers in envelopes that would ultimately be adhered to the back of Ford pick-up trucks. My parents said I worked for hours in front of the TV trying to see how big I could make my pile.

We kids always worked for my parents' companies. Then, at 14 years old, I started my first business named Diabetic Specialties, shortly after being diagnosed with Type 1 (Juvenile) Diabetes.

The diagnosis was sudden and completely out of left field. It all started after a semi-finals baseball game. It was really hot that day and I remember we lost the game and I wasn't too upset because it meant we wouldn't have to play a double header. That by itself was out of character because I've always been competitive.

I thought it was probably just the heat, so when my buddies asked if I wanted to go to the County Fair that evening I agreed to go. I was really thirsty but not hungry and I drank a lot of lemonade, which at the fairgrounds is code for mostly sugar with water and a squeeze or two of lemon. It wasn't long before I left because I wasn't having a good time and I was pretty sure I was coming down with something.

My dad was suspicious almost right away because diabetes ran in his family and while he didn't know a whole lot about it, he knew there were three main symptoms: going to the bathroom a lot, being very thirsty, and losing weight rapidly. My mom disagreed because she thought I was a healthy kid and was sure I had just caught a flu bug.

The first doctor my parents brought me to agreed with my mom and sent me home with instructions to drink 7up and get some rest. For a diabetic, drinking 7up was just about the worst thing I could have done, because of the high sugar content. After three days in which I got significantly worse each day and lost an unusual amount of weight for that short amount of time, my dad took me to another doctor who took one look at me and told my dad to get me to the hospital immediately!

What my dad didn't know at the time was that I was nearly in a diabetic coma. He had to carry me in to the emergency room where they were waiting for us to arrive because the doctor had called ahead.

After measuring my blood sugar, the medical team couldn't believe I was alive, much less semi-conscious. A healthy person's normal blood glucose level ranges from 80 – 120.[7] My blood glucose level was 1,600. They told my parents that typically doctors don't want a diabetic's blood sugar to get over 200; mine was 8 times higher. To this day it is the highest blood sugar ever recorded at the Holland Hospital.

To my parents' credit, they never made me feel like I was weak because of my disease. I lived my life as if I was as normal as the next guy. If anything, it gave me a reason to take more risks and really live life to the fullest.

One of my favorite quotes of all time, one that really resonates with me, is from the movie *Braveheart*. It says: "Every man dies, but not every man lives." These words are my motto for life. I'm not afraid to do what I think is right; say what I think needs saying, and more than anything, to follow the Lord. If God gives me a nudge, I want to follow it. When I die, I want everyone to know that I have truly lived for Christ. This is my dream, my quest. This is what God made me for and I won't let fear keep me from being the man He wants me to be.

Part of living is learning how to cope with disappointment and sorrow. I learned about these feelings when my parents divorced the summer before my senior year in high school. It was a difficult divorce for both of my parents and there is always collateral damage for children in the best of situations, which mine was not. Things took a challenging turn for me when I found myself living in a duplex without either parent during my senior year.

I don't harbor resentment towards either of my parents because they were both doing the best they could, but it turned my world upside down to go from what I felt was a solid family to feeling alone in the world. Eventually, two buddies moved in with me, which seemed like a good idea at the time. Looking back, I can see that it was a recipe for trouble, because we were all seventeen years old, living without our parents or boundaries.

Prior to my parents' divorce, I didn't drink alcohol. It was so far off my radar that I didn't even realize that I wasn't being invited to the parties. My brother Marc and I worked for my dad all throughout high school and I never had a lot of free time to wonder what everyone else was doing. My friends and Marc's friends worked for my dad along with us, so we never felt left out of the social scene.

But that all changed in a heartbeat when my buddies and I lived in the duplex that year. In short, we had a lot of fun and made a lot of mistakes, but God did protect us. We never got in trouble with the law or hurt anyone.

My friend's parents, some teachers, and even my principal protected me to varying degrees throughout that year. The parents always made sure I was okay and had enough to eat. They knew I was a diabetic and that things were going on in the duplex that probably weren't healthy for me. My teachers and principal protected me by calling me out when I got out of line. I think they probably cut me some slack because they had suspicions about my situation at home.

After high school, I worked full-time to put myself through college. To make money, I formed a partnership with a friend of mine while attending Western Michigan University. Together we started a new venture that tapped into some of my dad's contacts from the medical supply company that he owned at the time.

Our business was called Prime Medical and we manufactured and sold everything from commodes to walkers, but it ended up being walking canes that became our niche product.

The idea came about when I was in town one day and saw an older woman with an ugly aluminum cane. I thought, "wouldn't it be cool if she could have a cane to match every outfit?" We found a relatively new technique called powder coating, which sprays a "powdered" paint onto the part with an electrostatic spray gun. It's the electrostatic charge that makes it bond to the metal. When heated, it forms a super tough finish that doesn't chip, crack, or peel like traditional solvent based paints.

It's now the fastest growing painting method in the United States, but in the 1980's it wasn't as well known. Using this technique we could create any color cane that the customer wanted.

Prime Medical made a profit, but we were in college and easily sidetracked by girls, jet skiing, and just about anything that seemed fun. Clearly, we weren't as successful as we might have been if our work ethic had been better, but it was a great lesson in how *not* to run a business.

After graduating from college, we were lucky enough to sell the business to a huge company out of Chicago and got our investment back. I never ran a business half-heartedly again.

That's the way businesses have always started for me: I see a need and I don't fear taking a risk to go about finding a way to fill it. It's kind of like solving a puzzle. When my parents divorced, for example, my mom moved into a single-wide mobile home and we soon found that the roof needed coating so it wouldn't leak.

It was a miserably messy, hot, sticky, smelly job; but while I was up on her roof I looked around and saw that there were about a hundred other roofs, many of which were going to need to be coated as well. The next day I sent out flyers (I found out the hard way that you're not allowed to stick them in people's mailboxes) and within days my phone was ringing off the hook.

Eventually, I was able to buy in bulk from one distributer in town and, by keeping my costs to a minimum, I made a lot of money that summer.

The philosophy I subscribed to was one I called "business common sense." It's all about making the best use of the tools you have been given whether that is a mind for numbers, a talent for motivating people; or whatever your unique talent happens to be. I'm thankful that the Father gave me the ability to look at a situation, get a vision of how it could be and know what it's going to take to get there. Making that vision a reality also includes an element of faith because in order to achieve your dreams, you must be willing to take risks.

God gives us these talents and we can waste them or use them for good, but He leaves that choice up to us.

Shortly after college I met and married my wife Lisa, the mother of our two children: Torryn (Torry) Elise and Alexander (Alex) Todd. We were a traditional family in the sense that I worked outside the house and she worked at home taking care of our family. In other words, I was an accountant and she was the domestic engineer.

An opportunity to work with children happened while I was working as a Senior Accountant for Johnson Corporation in Three Rivers, Michigan.

Through my children and their friends, I saw there was a need for a mentorship program. A group of people from the community got together and created the Three Rivers Academic Mentoring program (TRAM). The goal was to bring the community together by pairing adults with 4th Grade at-risk students. We funded field trips where the kids could go on outings like a Detroit Tigers baseball game. With all of the activities, our number one goal was trying to provide a positive influence in the kid's lives.

A secondary hope was that the program would help to unify our community. It wasn't an earth-shattering new idea. TRAM came about because a few people wanted to make a difference and pulled the trigger to make it happen. There are so many people with fantastic ideas, but ideas by themselves won't help anyone. It just takes one person to say, "Hey, we can do this!" and then does it. When that happens, it will change your life forever.

A little boy named, Kevin Syzmanski, was one of the most inspiring people I've ever met. His courageous love of life reinforced my determination to push harder to impact lives.

Kevin's Gift

When I started biking, one thing that I learned quickly was that car-drivers typically don't like bikers. I saw some pretty bad car/bike wrecks as a result of drivers not paying attention. Texting can be deadly. A lot of broken bones and damaged bikes also resulted from bikers colliding with each other.

Bikers often ride in packs In order to benefit from 'drafting' behind the biker in front (less wind resistance resulting in less fatigue). If one bike collides with another, all of the bikes behind them start falling like dominos and you can literally hear the metal crunching through the shouts and surprised screeches from the riders.

Exhaustion is another huge factor in road accidents because, after some time biking, riders can lose focus and swerve in front of a car or another rider. I always enjoyed biking in spite of the hazards. For me it was competitive fun and a good way to stay in shape. It was a lot like a social event where everyone knew each other because the same people biked in the ride year after year.

I biked in the Dalmac ride for several years shortly after my son Alex was born. The Dalmac is a 4-Day, 330 mile ride that starts at the Michigan State University Pavilion in East Lansing, heads to the Mackinac Bridge, and ends at St Ignace in Michigan's Upper Peninsula.

Then, in 1996 I was invited to my first ride for the Make-A-Wish Foundation in a 200 mile course from the GM proving grounds in Detroit, to Frankenmuth, Michigan, and back. Two years later, I started to do this race regularly, because its purpose was to raise money for the Make-a-Wish kids.

Beginning in 1998, bikers started at the Mackinac Bridge and rode back to Detroit. At the end of each ride they have what's called the 'Hero's Hoorah' where the kids, their families and other spectators gather to cheer on the bikers as they reach the end of the race.

Once the riders crossed the finish line, one of the event volunteers would take our bikes, because after riding a bike for a hundred miles, we could hardly walk. Then a Make-A-Wish child would come up and put a medal around each of our necks.

When I crossed the finish line a very special blonde-haired, blue-eyed boy with Muscular Dystrophy named Kevin Syzmanski put the medal around my neck. He was a child who I later learned had literally touched thousands of lives through his and his family's work in the Make-A-Wish Foundation.

Kevin's parents, Lin and Dale Syzmanski, are probably the bravest parents I've ever met. Instead of raising him to feel he was handicapped, they started every day by asking "What are we going to do today?" Kevin and I had a lot in common. One was that our favorite part of these events was the Hero's Hoorah. He loved it and really got into the ceremonious presentation of the medal. If the organizers would let him, he would have presented a medal to every rider.

I remember that day like it was yesterday. I was very touched by the ironic symbolism of the medals being given by the Make-A-Wish children because those kids were the real heroes. As soon as he put the medal around my neck, Kevin started firing off questions. His mom, Lin, told me that

Kevin was at a stage where he could ask a hundred questions in one sitting if the person would let him. And I did. I think we talked for two hours the day we met!

Kevin asked question after question about my bike: How fast does it go? What kind of bike is it? What is this equipment for? I patiently answered every question the best I could and I enjoyed our time every bit as much as he did.

Kevin and Todd, at the end of a Make-A-Wish ride
(Kevin already has Todd's gloves)

Then Kevin threw me for a loop with his next question, asking if he could ride my bike. Here was a kid in a wheelchair who clearly did not have the strength to ride a bike, but he was asking me as if it was the most natural thing in the world. I didn't know how to tell him "no", so I said something like, "Oh, I think this bike is a little too big for you."

It was a lame answer, but the best I could come up with at the moment. Then, when I had satisfied all of his questions for the moment and was getting ready to leave, I asked if he wanted my hat and biking gloves. It was a weird thing to ask, but Kevin loved it! From that point on, every time I came across the finish line at a Make-A-Wish event, I would give Kevin my hat and gloves.

Lin told me later that Kevin loved to get autographs of the bikers and wanted me to sign the gloves and hat I had given him. Sure enough, as I was walking away, Lin chased me down and asked if I would sign the gloves and the hat for Kevin. I took that opportunity to ask her about Kevin's condition. Lin told me that he could still walk in the pool because of the weightless effect of the water and he still had good basic functions. But he was getting weaker and was starting to lose weight, which signified the deterioration of his muscles and was confirmation of progression of his disease.

Afterwards, we went our separate ways to have something to eat and just enjoy the camaraderie of all the people at the event. I caught up to them before they left the event and handed Lin my business card. I really wanted her to write to me and tell me Kevin's story.

Lin said she would, and soon after the event I received the promised email explaining that she and her husband, Dale, adopted Kevin before he was diagnosed at 2 years old with Duchene Muscular Dystrophy. They had noticed that his gross motor skills didn't seem to be developing like other children his age, so they took him to a doctor to have it checked out.

Shortly after that first visit, they received the heart-breaking prognosis that Kevin had Duchene, which they learned was a progressive disease for which there is no cure. It was especially hard to accept because Kevin was such a beautiful and healthy-looking little boy.

Lin said, "All of Kevin's milestones were late... he never ran, couldn't ride a bike. The prognosis is morbidly described as, 'wheelchair by 10; gone by 20'. Kevin was in a wheelchair at 11 years old because I was too stubborn to let him get in a wheelchair at 10 years old."

It still chokes me up when I remember Lin telling me, "Kevin thought he would live forever. What I loved most about the interaction between you and Kevin was that you never treated him like he was challenged or sick; you treated him with love, respect, admiration & gentleness. And as he got older, you treated him like a man."

Kevin was girl crazy from the time he was about 12 or 13 years old, so that was definitely something we had in common, too. Lin would always roll her eyes and laugh when we took off to hang out like guys and check out the chicks.

The Syzmanski's became like family to me and my kids, and I remember how tough it was to see that effervescent little boy when he was in the hospital. His parent's told me that the doctors didn't think Kevin would make his 16th birthday because of a heart condition he had recently developed. Dale and Lin felt it was really important to have people celebrate his life while he was here, not after he passed. So, when he made it to 17 years old, they threw a big birthday party and invited anyone who had been a part of his life.

Kevin died in 2008, two weeks after his 21st birthday, but he lived more in 21 years than most people do in their entire lives. I always felt we were kindred spirits in a lot of ways. I had a picture of him in a frame that said, "INSPIRE" because that's what he did for me and so many others.

After Kevin's death, I invited the Syzmanski's to my house and didn't know what to make of it when I saw Lin start to cry. I didn't know what to do. Men are awful when women cry and it causes one of the most frustratingly helpless feelings for me. But Lin's tears were from happiness. She had seen the frame with Kevin's picture in it and realized she had always thought of *me* as an inspiration for her son without seeing the bigger picture.

As Lin said, "Seeing Kevin's picture in that frame made me understand that he was an inspiration to others and that was the reason God put Kevin on this earth. It was a moment that overwhelmed me because suddenly everything was in perspective and I was so proud to have been his mom."

God brings people into our lives unexpectedly; sometimes for a long time and sometimes just for a season, but regardless of the length of time these special people leave indelible marks on our hearts. His mom was right—the number of lives he touched and the way he inspired others was Kevin's real gift. To this very day, I have the bracelet with Kevin's name on it wrapped around the handle bars of my bike. Wherever I ride, whether in the United States, South Africa, or another part of the world, Kevin's inspiration reminds me to live with courage and deliberate joy.

Life Undefined

At this time in my life, supporting my family was my primary focus, and I couldn't see the toll that my absence was taking on my marriage. I guess it's true when people say that you can't put an old head on young shoulders, because I look back thinking, "If I just knew then what I know now."

I loved my family but I was also young, hungry, ambitious, and business was fun for me. I was home in the evenings the majority of the time. But instead of dividing my time between my wife and my children, my focus was always on the kids. Friends and family nicknamed me, "Mr. Mom", from the 80's movie because when I wasn't working I was playing with Alex and Torry. Whether it was coaching sports, teaching them how to ride a bike, or just carrying them around as babies in a backpack while I mowed the lawn, they were always with me.

As with most divorces, there were other issues; but in 12 years of marriage, I never actually thought that we wouldn't be able to forgive each other and save our marriage. It was devastating when I found myself in the same position my parents had been in 20 years earlier. My daughter Torry was very young and doesn't remember this difficult time, but Alex was older and unfortunately remembers the arguments and tension that could be cut with a knife.

The most difficult part of the divorce, besides the guilt and feelings of failure, was the physical separation from my children. Nothing I've ever experienced equals that type of gut-wrenching longing to be a part of their lives. I went from being 'Mr. Mom' to 'Mr. Weekend Dad,' a painful adjustment that I never felt at peace with; but I found that with passage of time comes a degree of acceptance.

Without a doubt, it brought my priorities into focus and I vowed I would never put business ahead of my family again.

At this time, I was living in a suburb of Detroit, Michigan, and had started a business called Global Business Synergy with nothing but an idea and a former colleague who believed in the idea enough to bring in investors. It was also during this time that I met Tom and Peg Woodside through the church we all attended. Tom and Peg were the couple that invited me on the trip to Ecuador where we held a Christmas Party in the Dump and I made my "deal" with God about providing the funds to enclose the little church in the Andes Mountains.

A year later, my life became more challenging when my children moved with their mother to Florida. Having them removed even further from my life was much harder than I anticipated. I managed by focusing on growing my business, but I made a promise to myself and to Alex and Torry that I would always be there for them whenever they needed me.

It was shortly after my children moved to Florida that I relocated my company's headquarters to Denver, Colorado. Only one short year after the "deal" with God, I was blessed beyond what I could have imagined. The company had flourished into a multi-million dollar organization and I was able to buy out the initial investors and rebrand the company as GB Synergy.

I had more money than I knew what to do with. That gave me the freedom to hop on a plane at a moment's notice to be with my children. I found myself learning to adjust to the jet-set relationship with my kids.

My life became a whirlwind. I remarried within mere months after relocating to Denver, and managed to keep my promise to Torry and Alex that they would be my priority without neglecting my responsibility to my wife. The teachers got a kick out of this crazy dad who would fly thousands of miles from Denver to Florida for a Parent-Teacher conference. I racked up a lot of airline miles flying myself, Alex, and Torry back and forth from Florida to Denver. More than anything, I felt closer to them by staying involved in their day-to-day lives.

We all cope in different ways and I found myself turning more and more to my faith for direction. I'll be honest, learning to let go of control and handing direction over to Jesus was not something that came easily for me. My new wife had a relationship with the Lord that I wanted to achieve and she gave me opportunities to grow closer to God through Bible studies we held at our house.

I never expected to feel so full of joy and contentment from having a faith centered life. The more I grew spiritually, the more I craved having an even closer walk with the Lord. And I wanted others to know the same joy.

People say that enthusiasm has never been something I lack. In fact, friends have rolled their eyes at that comment and finished the statement saying that more often than not I have too many ideas and need to be reined in. We all have our shortcomings, and passion happens to be both my greatest strength and perhaps my greatest weakness.

I'm not sure if being a diabetic freed me to take more risks or if I took more risks to prove that the disease was not going to define me. Regardless, I want to inspire the same desire to live with a "Go Big" attitude towards helping others in the name of Jesus.

Anonymity Shrugged

For me, creating Barnabas was a lot like going into a mansion for the first time. You can stand in the foyer with eyes wide open and see the doors to all of the rooms, but you can't see inside them. The longer you live in that house, the more familiar you become, and eventually, you will be able to stand in the same foyer and see the entire house in your mind's eye.

Starting Barnabas Charities meant I had stepped into the metaphorical foyer by following God's lead. When Barnabas Charities was first organized as a 501C-3 organization, it was an anonymous charity. All gifts were accompanied by a card and encouraging scripture signed with the charity name without identifying an individual or even giving an address. Checks only had the charity name and our slogan, "Facilitating God's Love," printed on them.

Enthusiasm is contagious. It quickly spread to the employees of GB Synergy who indicated they wanted to get involved, so we set up a program for them to contribute to Barnabas Charities. It was great to be successful at business, but to be doing work to make a difference in people's lives—that was the real deal! Serving others resonated with my soul so much that I felt exuberance and clarity of purpose like never before.

Life was good. I was madly in love, the relationship with my kids had settled into a consistently chaotic way of life, and professionally I was at the top of my game—but that didn't mean I was becoming complacent. The money made my mind race with ideas for finding ways to make Barnabas reach more people.

After Katrina hit and I made the trip to New Orleans, the desire within me grew stronger than ever before. A week after returning from the trip, I felt called to return to New Orleans and continue to help with the effort to relocate people who were stranded in the shelters. This time there was no hesitation.

While continuing from home to match up people in the shelters, I was put in touch with a bus company out of Colorado Springs that agreed to provide a fleet of buses for the relief effort. As before, it seemed the pieces were all falling together right before my eyes.

I had a travel-mate once again when my neighbor, Diane Beede, agreed to accompany me on the second trip. Mark and Diane Beede went to the same church and I knew that Diane had expressed a desire to go on a mission trip; so when I felt God calling me back to New Orleans, I asked if she wanted to go.

Diane brought a fresh new perspective to the trip, not just because of her nursing background, but because she genuinely loves helping people. There was no doubt God was orchestrating the trip because in a normal situation Diane would not have been able to take off time from nursing work on such short notice. As a nurse, her shifts typically ran for 12 hours at a time. The chance of getting time off work was even more of a stretch because this was a new job for Diane.

When she asked about taking the time off, her boss surprised her, saying, "You have to go, Diane! We have talked about wanting to do something to help the people in New

Orleans and this will be our way of helping. Don't worry, we'll find a way to cover your shifts." And that was all there was to it. Her way had been cleared to come along with me on this second journey.

Mark was supportive of his wife, but he had some legitimate concerns about his wife going to New Orleans. We were sitting outside reminiscing about the first trip when Mark told us that he was both scared and elated when they decided that Diane was going to join him on the trip.

I remember his complex line of reasoning. He said:

> We knew Todd really well and we knew his heart, so we had faith that if he said he had a calling to go down to New Orleans to help, it didn't matter if he had a clear plan; Diane and I just knew things would fall into place. I was really excited for her to go because one of her gifts is nursing. So I thought there was an opportunity for her down there to put her skills to work and really do something good. On the other hand, if you watched the news, there were some regions that were extremely unstable and downright dangerous. I also knew it was going to be a grueling trip because Todd had an agenda and no obstacles were going to get in the way of making the trip successful!

We were ready to get moving. The bus company from Colorado Springs wanted to make a "test run" trip to check things out and asked if one of their employees could come along as well. We hadn't met the representative and we both were expecting someone around our age, so we were surprised when the bus company's representative was dropped off by her mother and we learned she was only 22 years old.

Having been there once already, I knew how raw everything was after the hurricane and that the suffering was difficult to handle. There are many 22 year olds who would be mature enough to handle the devastation of New Orleans at this time; unfortunately she wasn't one of them.

As the trip got underway we were practically sitting on the supplies because donations came in droves once the word got out that we were going back to New Orleans.

It was around 2 a.m. when Diane took over the wheel so I could get a little sleep before getting back to working on our agenda for the trip. All of a sudden Diane said, "Oh no, Todd! I'm getting pulled over for speeding!" I shot up and I whipped my head around to look back and sure enough, there were blue and red lights flashing. I wasn't upset at all, because once you see the lights flashing there's not much you can do anyway. Maybe it was the sleepiness, but it struck me as funny. We gave each other a smile like two kids who just got caught with their hand in a cookie jar as she pulled over to the side of the road.

When the police officer walked up to the vehicle he couldn't help but notice the supplies crammed in to every nook and cranny of the vehicle. So after checking our licenses and registration, he asked if we were headed to New Orleans. Diane smiled and told him we were and apologized for her lead foot. He said, "Look, I'm going to let you go with a warning, but slow down and just be aware of drunk drivers and cows."

We both thought, "Did he really just say cows?" Oh man, we didn't dare look at each other! It was like one of those times when you're sitting in church with a friend and you get the giggles. Your eyes start to water as you try not to laugh. Meanwhile you're getting a look from your parents up in the choir that says, "Don't even start!" And if the other person so much as snickers you're both done for and the laughter bubbles out uncontrollably. The moment the police officer was gone we both burst out laughing. All the way down it became a silliness trigger anytime one of us said, "Hey watch out for the cows!" and we would both start laughing all over again.

I'd done this trip before, so I told Diane it was going to be pretty easy. Famous last words. When we arrived I was all gung-ho and said, "Okay! Let's get started." But the bus company's representative was an emotional wreck as soon as she saw the shelters. We couldn't do anything but try to comfort her, because she had a difficult time coping when she saw the devastation firsthand.

We were relieved when a volunteer, who was helping with the shelter, took the bus representative under her wing. The volunteer showed her other shelters and explained how things worked so she would be able to convey the information back to her employer at the bus company.

The neat thing was to see God's hand at work in the situation. Later on, through the young lady from the bus company, I ended up working with her mother's mission project. The bus representative's mom worked at a women's correctional facility and had created a mission program to provide blankets to children in third world countries. They chose different areas around the world, so I asked her if they would be interested in sending some blankets to South Africa.

Many people think of South Africa as hot, and it is in the summer months. But winter temperatures can dip into the 40's and colder. In a place where children don't have shoes and share one worn blanket with their entire family, blankets were precious gifts.

In return, pictures were taken of the children holding their blankets and sent back to the correctional facility for the inmates to see that they had made a difference. The women created a wall of the pictures in the prison. It's a wonderful ministry that blessed many people by giving the women something positive to do during their incarceration along with the gift of knowing that a child would sleep warm because of their work.

Back in Alexandria, Diane and I sighed in relief when the bus representative was taken off our hands, which was quickly followed with a collective, "let's get down to business!" I really thought it would be easy to pick up where Eric and I had left off. But everywhere we went, we hit a brick wall.

The Red Cross wouldn't let us help unless we knew someone in the shelter and of course we didn't know a single soul. At first the rule seemed ridiculous to us, because if someone knew them, they wouldn't be in a shelter in the first place. We were literally *chased* out of shelters.

Our story was relayed back to Pueblo and Denver where the local papers reported on the situation. The story was then picked up by the Associated Press who wrote:

> The leader of a grass roots effort to bring Hurricane Katrina families to Colorado said the effort has been bogged down by red tape.
>
> The Red Cross says it also has a responsibility to give evacuees as much privacy as they can in their new temporary home, give them time to think about what they want to do next, and get connected with the government so they can receive emergency aid.

A spokesman for the Red Cross in Denver said groups that want to help can drop off brochures explaining what they can do to help and they will pass that information on to evacuees to consider.

"We're not keeping anyone prisoner. We just will not allow anyone in who hasn't been invited," he said. "I think the easiest thing is going to be getting them into a home." [8]

Saying the *easiest* thing was going to be getting evacuees in a home is about as rational as a unicorn in pajamas. If it was "the easiest thing," why were the shelters so full of people?

Later we understood that the people running the shelters weren't making the decisions and must have felt they were protecting the evacuees. Perhaps they were, but many of the evacuees told us later that they felt confined rather than protected. At one shelter armed guardsmen were ordered to escort women onto one bus and men onto another bus to take them to a facility to shower. Then, they were returned to the shelter by armed escort. When they arrived back at the shelter, they were frisked and run through metal detectors.

Evacuees told us that it was like they were criminals and many felt as if the 'system' was hindering instead of helping the process. To be honest, we could understand why the shelters had rules not allowing strangers on the premises because, sadly, there are many who would prey upon people in such a vulnerable situation.

I started to question why God brought me back if every door was going to be shut in our faces. It had been a long drive and we were tired and discouraged, so I suggested we go back to the hotel and get some dinner. Over dinner we were rehashing the day when the light bulb went on and I suddenly had a clear understanding about why things weren't going well. We were following our plan instead of God's plan. I thought I had everything figured out when all along God had been telling us, "Hey guys, you really do need me."

Right then and there we prayed, "Lord, we were wrong. We were trying to do things our way. When we wake up tomorrow, please guide us to do your will and to see what you would have us do and serve as you would have us serve."

We woke up to a gloriously beautiful day and I felt a completely different energy. I was determined to follow God instead of trying to do things my own way. I wasn't quite sure how I would know the difference but I was going to try.

When we went up to the front desk in the morning before heading out to see if we had any messages, we were given a note that someone had called saying they needed transportation to a family member. That was awesome. I felt certain this was my first instruction, so I made a couple of quick calls and was connected with an organization called Angel Wings who acted as a "matchmaker," connecting people who had a compelling need for transportation but couldn't afford it, with people willing to get them home.

After that, the doors just opened to us. Red Cross let us into the shelter and we just started talking to people. Some people only wanted prayers. Others needed a little assistance for small things, so we gave them cash to help. Then we started matching people with families all over the country, in addition to those who were going to travel back to Denver with us on the bus. It was awesome to do something to help and to feel that every bit of love we gave was returned.

What we saw in the shelters varied. A consistently terrible condition we witnessed was the food being served. We wondered aloud where all the billions being funneled into the relief effort were going, because it wasn't being spent on providing decent food to the shelters we visited.

One shelter housed evacuees in an abandoned Safeway grocery store. They were serving disgusting food, so we decided to get a hot chicken dinner for everyone in the shelter. We cleaned out the local Kentucky Fried Chicken and brought the food back to the shelter.

When we arrived, one of the workers asked, "What do you have there?" Diane told them we brought chicken dinner for everyone. With a big smile, the man walked over to a big trash bin, dragged it to the end of the table, stretched his arm out and pushed all of the food they had set out into the garbage can.

At another shelter, an older man was disgusted with the food he had to serve. When we asked how we could help the man replied, "If you really want to help, you can buy me a grill so I can cook for these people. The food isn't fit for dogs!" So we bought the man a grill. He started grinning from ear to ear. We knew he was going to have a ball cooking and the people in that shelter were going to eat well. The man told Diane, "This is one of those acts of kindness you don't forget."

Meanwhile, back in Denver, parents were getting their children involved by asking what they could donate to the kids relocating to their town from New Orleans. It was great to see the generosity the kids demonstrated as they donated toys, skateboards, Nintendo DS, and everything in-between.

Loading the bus for Colorado Springs

After returning home and having a chance to reflect on the experience, I realized that as a Christian, my plans aren't anything and God's plans are everything. To submit to His will and follow His plans, and then witness how doors start opening—it was amazing. It's the first time I'd ever experienced God that powerfully.

Diane shared her thoughts, saying, "Todd was an example of someone who had the best intentions, but learned he can't follow his own plans. He had to humble himself, listen for God's direction and follow His plan." I just had to chuckle and shake my head because she had me pegged with her insight.

That trip back to New Orleans was a life-changing month. I now knew two things for certain: First, I was committed to changing the focus of Barnabas Charities from one that provided help to individuals or families anonymously, to an organization that can make a difference on a large scale. The second clarity was that I wanted to do Barnabas work full-time. Business no longer held the appeal that it had for my entire life up to this point.

I had wealth, an exquisite home, my children, good friends, a loving wife and faith that grew with each new step. There was an incredible amount of need out in the world around me and a lot of good intentioned people who want to help but can't quite get past the "wanting" to actually taking action. So I started to think of how Barnabas Charities could provide a way for ordinary Christians like me to be involved in specific projects.

The plan started to unfold as I began to understand that, if I am truly submitting to God's calling, it may not always be the choice that I would make, but the choice God has made for me. And God knows obedience is not something that comes easy for me. I'm in His remedial program, learning this lesson over and over again.

Seriously, God has such a wonderful way of putting experiences in our paths to prepare us for the next adventure in our journey as Christians. After the two trips to New Orleans, the people who relocated to La Junta, Pueblo, Colorado Springs, and Denver wanted to thank us by cooking an authentic New Orleans dinner.

We gathered at my house for the celebration, so I invited the whole group to come to our church on Sunday before the feast. Our minister, Pastor Kevin, said he had never preached with such energy as he did that day and let me tell you, they knew how to worship! It was contagious when they sang and shouted, "Preach It, Preacher!!" There were loud "Amen's" and "Yes, Jesus!" I think half of the congregation was in culture shock but I'll never forget it because our church was so full of God's presence that day.

Then everyone went back to my house and cooked jambalaya, crawfish, dirty rice, and all the fixin's for a New Orleans dinner. It was a feast and praise session all rolled up into one! I stepped back to soak it all in. While I was watching everyone laugh and talk to their new friends with a relaxed happiness on their faces, I felt peacefulness settle over me. It was confirmation of God's calling for me to get out there.

I still felt scattered about my direction, but I didn't have to wait long before He started to fit the pieces together.

Diane Beede & her family, with a family moving from New Orleans to Denver

Catalyst

The opening of a deep interest in Africa took place not long after I returned from the second trip to Louisiana. My wife and I had gone to the *Catalyst Conference* with our friends Mark and Diane. It was the largest gathering of Christian youth and leaders in the country. A stadium was literally filled with groups of people who came from around the country to worship together during this three day event.

Catalyst has amazing speakers, chart-topping musicians and vendor booths manned by innovators and people making change around the world.

I spent a lot of time at the Africa booth. I had been thinking of Africa a lot lately and wondered if God had placed in my heart a desire to go there. I was at the point in my faith where I was trying to follow God's lead, but didn't always know if it was my desire or what He was telling me to do. Then Diane Beede (the friend and neighbor who also went with me on the second Katrina trip) laughed as she said, "It was no coincidence. Todd just kept going back to the booth, over and over. Mark and I could almost hear the wheels grinding in his head."

It was true. I was fired up after going to the Africa booth, which was all about getting water to villages that didn't have wells to provide fresh drinking water. I talked to the leaders to get an idea about what kind of raw materials they already had, talked about the facilities that were already in place and how the pricing worked. This project seemed to be a great fit for what I hoped to be able to do through Barnabas.

My direction was getting clear, but God hadn't revealed *how* I was going to find the time to run my business and run Barnabas on the other side of the world at the same time. Thinking about it now, I can imagine God was looking down on me and shaking his head, smiling much like a parent would when telling their child to just be patient.

Instead of feeling overwhelmed, all I felt was enthusiasm for this project. The plan came together pretty quickly from there and the group who hosted the booth felt the direction had changed from "Wow, this is a cool idea!" to "Wow! We can really do this!" I prayed that God would make it clear to me that my calling to Africa was His plan for me.

I had been turning different scenarios around in my mind when I settled on one that I decided to share with my wife. It would require us to work as a team more than ever, but it was something we could make work because our marriage was strong. What made it so strong was that we were colleagues, mutually supportive, and devoted to each other.

I knew she had a strong desire to run GB Synergy. Owning and running her own business was a dream she had nurtured since before graduating from college. She was a 5% owner of GB Synergy and was privy to virtually unlimited information about the business through our marriage. Besides being the best JD Edwards trainer I'd ever met, my wife knew our business inside and out.

But the quality that I felt made her a strong leader was her faith. I'd never met a woman who knew more about the Bible or who had a closer relationship with the Lord. She had even preached at our church on a couple occasions. Because of the love and trust in our marriage, we agreed that I would turn over the role of GB Synergy CEO to her, which would free me up to run Barnabas full time. I can't tell you how excited we both were to be able to follow our dreams!

The next piece of the puzzle fell into place when a man named Ron Cline invited my wife and me to travel as part of a mission team to South Africa. Jerry Carnill knew I was interested in looking at potential projects in Africa, so when he learned that Ron and Barb Cline were going to take a team he suggested they ask us to come along.

Ron and his wife Barb led the mission trip in December 2005. Ron was the President of HCJB radio station, whose fundamental mission is to spread the Gospel in native languages all throughout the world by radio. Many areas can have Christian worship in public, while in other parts of the world people risk their lives to learn about Jesus. In those areas, HCJB radio essentially becomes their "church." People could gather as a congregation to listen to the teachings of the Bible in private locations. Making the Word available through their global radio ministry has been a powerful achievement.

There were 18 people in our group and we stayed in a place called the ACTS Team House, which was located in Fish Hoek, right outside of Cape Town, South Africa. The people on this trip were great. We would get up at 6 a.m., have devotions at 7 a.m., be done with breakfast and be out the door by 8 a.m. ready for the day's work. We'd come home in the evening for supper, and by 10 p.m., most people were ready for bed. I was always too wound up to go to sleep. Fortunately there were others who felt the same because we stayed up most of the night, debriefing about the day, and sometimes just talking about life in general.

It became a routine for me to have breakfast with my good friends from Detroit, Michigan, Tom and Peg Woodside. They were in the group that went to bed around 10 p.m., so we talked every morning and I shared ideas that had come up in conversations the night before. At times, ideas from those talks were used to plan the activities for the days ahead. I loved the people and it was amazing how close we all became in such a short period of time.

The first night in South Africa, Ron Cline was leading a group discussion about salvation, randomly calling on people to share their salvation story. I was sweating bullets. I listened a bit cynically to everyone talking about how they were saved at church camp or at Sunday school or at the conclusion of a Sunday service at 12 years old. I felt like a kid who didn't want to be called on by the teacher in class, trying not to make eye contact, hoping the teacher wouldn't notice me. But it didn't work. Sure enough Ron called on me, asking if I would share my salvation story.

Later, Ron told me that he could see I was nervous about sharing my story, but it wasn't uncommon for people to be a little uncomfortable talking about this topic at first. He said, "You paid attention to everything and I found myself wondering where you stood spiritually. I knew you were out doing great work with children, but I didn't know where you stood spiritually so I called on you to share with the group."

The trouble was that I didn't know how to express where I was. Shortly before leaving for this trip, I came to terms with something that I have carried with me most of my life— feelings of shame. After a couple years of Christian counseling, I dealt with these feelings in a healthy way and for the first time in a very long time, I was free.

Until I dealt with those feelings, I didn't fully know what it meant to walk with Jesus. I was terrified when Ron Cline called on me to share my salvation story. I wanted to be authentic, but I wasn't ready, so I said that I would share, but asked if it was okay if I speak with him first. I could see Ron was puzzled for the blink of an eye, but then he smiled and said, "Sure you can."

Then he moved on to another person in the group. Later when he saw me, he asked if it was a good time to talk and we went to speak in private.

I told him about the situation I was trying to come to terms with and described my serious questions about what it meant to be 'saved'. Sure, I could say I was saved when I was 12 or 13 at church like everyone else in the room. The truth was I didn't fully understand what salvation really meant back then.

I'd always thought I was a Christian, but I didn't realize until that year what it really meant. It took me almost 40 years, but I finally got it.

Ron encouraged me to share my story with the group. He was leaving it up to me but he said he thought I needed to do it. I knew he wouldn't embarrass me and that the decision was mine to make, so I gave Ron the green light to call on me. When the time came I shared my personal salvation story. I probably didn't make sense to most of the people in the room, but it was a pivotal moment in my life nonetheless.

Ron remembered that event, saying:

> It was necessary for Todd to say it out loud, and it was necessary for the team to hear him. Todd's testimony was pretty disjointed because he was going back and forth as he remembered, but he did a good job and

the team sure appreciated the authenticity of his message. He got choked up and humbled himself in tears. I knew he wasn't the type of man who cried a lot so it was a big deal. I think it was pretty clear at that point that Todd needed to do something more serious with his life than making money.

The group was very supportive. They laid their hands on me and prayed. I felt surrounded with encouragement, reinforcement, and love. I was part of this team, so I was part of the family. Teams are like that. They live together, work together; you don't know each other the first day, but by the second or third day you're doing things together that you never dreamed you would do.

After the meeting, Ron's wife Barb talked to the team and said:

> You know every one of us has our own "shame" that we carry around with us. Let's take it down to the beach and bury it in the sand. Put it to rest forever. God doesn't want us to carry these burdens around with us. That's why he sent Jesus so we could be forgiven and lay our burdens at his feet.

I decided to ask the Woodsides if they would go down to the beach with my wife and me. On the way down we found a rock and picked it up. The rock was a physical representation of mistakes I had made that I'd been carrying around for years. The physical act of burying that rock and then all of us praying together afterwards was cathartic for me and I gave all of it to God.

It was a beautifully clear night and before returning to the house we stayed on the beach a little longer just looking up at the stars. Tom knew quite a bit about astronomy and he noticed something special in the heavens that night. Pointing to a group of stars he exclaimed, "Hey, look up there! Now this is something you don't see every day, it's the Southern Cross!" He explained that you can only see this constellation in the Southern Hemisphere and it's about as prominent as the big dipper is in the Northern Hemisphere.

We were all looking up in the direction of the Southern Cross. And as we stood there we saw this extraordinary shooting star angled right through the middle of the center of the cross. It was the brightest shooting star I've ever seen, and it had a huge arc. It was a perfect cloudless night. There is no doubt we were in God's presence and I don't think any of us will ever forget it. It was like God was saying, "Yeah, I'm really here with you." It was an amazing experience.

The rest of the trip was a joy for all of us. Tom and Peg thought I was like a kid because I was fired up and had so many ideas bouncing around in my head. Thankfully, they kept my feet planted on the ground. Peg is a wonderful woman and a dear friend. Having said that, she has also called me her "problem child" once or twice, but I know it's said with love. It's hard to be credible describing ourselves to others, so here's what Peg has to say:

> Todd doesn't care if other people think he's silly. He would just start dancing and get a bunch of kids dancing with him. I'd be too embarrassed to just get up there, but he has tremendous joy in his spirit. He was the leader of the band, the Pied Piper. The kids would just follow him around everywhere and he loved it!

I remember one time a group of little kids were sitting around with Todd and they started wrestling in the dirt. There were about 7 kids against Todd. It's just like him to do something like that. Another time, we brought a Slip-N-Slide with us and we put a little soap on it to make it really slippery. Todd just thought it looked like too much fun, so he joined in and the kids were rolling on the ground laughing when they saw him go down that slide!

I wasn't always an adolescent. There were quiet times when Ron and I would talk. He encouraged me to follow my heart with Barnabas. I asked Ron how I would know, when I feel moved to go in a certain direction, whether it is God's will or just something I want to do? Ron replied, "You just do it. If what you are doing is God's will then the doors will just keep opening. If it's not, the doors will close."

Ron shares a bit of what we talked about in terms of Barnabas and the work to change lives in South Africa:

Todd wanted to do what we were doing. Now, you need to know Jerry Carnill serves full time with Extreme Response, so he's constantly doing that. My son Russ works full time with Leader Mundial, and he's constantly interfacing with people on the ground in South Africa. I'm full time with HCJB and I get to do this day-in and day-out; so Todd's kind of exposed to all three of us and he's saying, "I want to do that!"

A challenging dynamic is presented when you take a person who is used to being the CEO of a company that he created, is used to being able to make things happen on his timetable, and then you take away that control. It's going to be easy for him to become frustrated and I think that will be the biggest hurdle he has to overcome.

My timing and God's timing—those are two clocks that don't always chime at the same hour. It really wouldn't matter if I was a business owner or not. The same struggles could be had by a teacher, homemaker, mechanic, or engineer. Many, many of us struggle with giving up control. It takes practice and discipline for me because it's something I understand intellectually, but my heart has a hard time accepting. Until that happens, it is as if God's saying, "Nope, you're not ready yet." And that sometimes frustrates me, too.

I believe it's because God leads his children along in different ways and he usually doesn't show us the end before He takes us there. It's during those times we learn about faith. The basic rule, as it relates to anyone who's trying to build God's Kingdom, is you have to get out of God's way and let God do it.

It takes a lot of faith and a lot of willingness to deal with your own personal pride and sense of importance. It takes a willingness to do what needs to be done. Everyone, and I do mean everyone, has to work on it on a daily basis. You can't take one of these trips and go out there with a pre-set agenda and say, "This is what I want to do." because that's not what you're going to do most of time. That's just the way it works in missions. We think God needs us. We just need to get out of His way.

This is Who We Are

"It looked like Beirut. It seriously looked like a bomb must have gone off. There were no people, just utter devastation. We arrived at the house and I remember thinking to myself, 'This must be what Hell looks like.' It was beyond bad," said my friend, Katrina Golden after seeing the 8th and 9th Wards in New Orleans a year after Hurricane Katrina.

A lot of the iconic images depicting the destruction wrought by Katrina were taken of this area in New Orleans; especially the images seen on the television news stations. What remained after the waters receded was horrifying.

The National Guard had gone through each of the houses. On the outside of each house was a big X. In the top quadrant of the X was a number representing the date the home was searched. The bottom quadrant of the X has another number, representing the number of dead found in the house. The right quadrant noted any hazards such as gas, water tanks, or dead animals found. Finally, the left quadrant of the X showed the initials of the search squad that went through the house.

Katrina Golden said, "Every single house in the 9th Ward had one of these X's. When you saw a house with a larger number in the bottom quadrant of the X, you knew a whole family had been found in that house. Everyone silently hoped for houses with zeros. We went by an apartment complex that had a big number on it and I can't even begin to describe the bone deep grief we all felt."

One man who lived in the 9th Ward heard the levies break, he literally saw the water coming and lived to tell about it. The man was on his front porch talking with his cousin when they heard a tremendous noise and then saw the water rushing toward them. It was like something out of the movies, except this was really happening and his home was only about two blocks from the levy! His actions were instinctive and fueled by adrenaline; the time for being terrified would come later.

The man quickly told his cousin to go into the house and get everyone on the roof. Then he ran across the street to his aunt's house and told them to do the same, shouting to anyone who could hear him over the roar of the water as he went. He made it across the street and into the house, but couldn't get back because the water rushed in so quickly and with such force. Whatever wasn't anchored down was swept away.

Katrina told me this story with a mixture of compassion and frustration, explaining that the man asked her to bring their story back to others because many people in the 8th and 9th Wards felt as if they had been forgotten. The newness of the disaster had worn off and people wanted to get back to their lives; they didn't want to see the heartbreak of what still remained a year later. The man's young son was standing by his side all the while he was talking to Katrina. When his dad finished, the boy looked up at Katrina and said with pride in his voice, "My dad saved our neighbors."

Those five words spoken by that child put everything into perspective for me. We are to care for one another. That's our job and that's what I brought my children here to learn.

It was now August 2006, nearly a year after the hurricane ravaged New Orleans, and a daunting amount of work still needed to be done. People were living in tiny FEMA trailers because their homes, if they still had a home, needed to be torn down to the studs and rebuilt. Looking at the devastation with my own eyes, it didn't seem as if FEMA had even made a dent.

The opportunity to bring Alex and Torry down to Louisiana was presented when I received an unexpected call from Katrina Golden asking if I wanted to go on a trip to help with the rebuilding effort in New Orleans. God hooked us up originally when we didn't know each other from a can of paint, so it was awesome to be able to work on a project together a year after the storm.

When I asked her about bringing Alex and Torry, Katrina said it would be okay but she let me know in no uncertain terms that it wouldn't be a vacation and they should come prepared to work. Katrina had brought other groups of students to volunteer their time for the rebuilding effort in the past, so she felt that my kids would be okay.

Alex and Torry knew that I had gone to Ecuador, New Orleans, and South Africa on mission trips and thought I was working to do good things for people, but I wanted them to take that step themselves. We are the hands and feet of God and I wanted my children to know the joy of helping others.

Our job was to gut a house for a woman named Laura Hochberger, who cared for her elderly father-in-law and her disabled husband. There was another group that would follow to rebuild the house but before the other team could begin the structural work, the house had to be completely cleared out.

It was July in the South and it was exhausting to stand still. The air was thick with humidity, and the smell was an acrid stench of rot and mold that collided with us as soon as we entered the Hochberger's home. As we walked through and looked around it was unsettling, even *creepy*, to see the state of the house. All of the furniture was just where it was left before the flood; except now it was moldy and ruined. I remember thinking, "They lost everything." And it was clear that when they said we had to empty the house, they meant to the studs! Everything had to go.

Our crew consisted of Katrina, Alex, Torry, a man who came down on his own from Minnesota, and me. The purpose for walking through the house was to determine a plan of attack. You could tell how high the water was because it left behind a black line on the walls where it settled and stayed for a period of time before receding further. The water had probably been to the roof, but the first waterline was about 5 feet high. A foot or so down there was another waterline where the water had receded and then sat for awhile again. These waterlines were like the lines in a sedimentary stone that marked the passage of time by the layers in the rock.

People didn't have time to clean up or put things in storage when they were told to evacuate, so whatever was in the house when they left was still there after the storm: furniture, dishes, food, bedding, drapes, carpeting. Except now everything had been cooked in stagnant water and 110 degree heat.

I remember seeing wood furniture knocked over and the varnish peeling off like a snake shedding its skin after being soaked in water for days. It looked and smelled like a dump.

The stench was a combination of sewer odors, food that had gone bad, and the powerful smell of mold that was everywhere. The humidity amplified the stench to a point where anyone working in the house had to wear a special mask to avoid inhaling the harmful mold spores, but it did little to disguise the smell.

We couldn't have done this job on our own. God put it in our hearts and gave us the strength to see it through. I had a moment of worry because while Alex was sixteen, Torry was only thirteen. Katrina teased me about this time saying, "You say I'm a force of nature? You were busier than me: directing, cheering people on. You had us all working hard and cracking up with laughter at the same time."

Alex hauling out a load of debris

We started in the room closest to the front door, and then began taking everything out to the curb. The city came by periodically to pick up the refuse and haul it to the dump. One by one, every house had to be gutted. It was an extraordinary amount of work and the sheer manual labor was much more difficult than we anticipated because of the heat.

I was proud of the work Alex and Torry did on that home. Wearing a muscle shirt, shorts and work boots, at 6' 2" and around 175 lbs, Alex was a big sixteen year old kid. He tore down and hauled load after load out of the house. He worked like a champ without ever complaining about the conditions. Torry worked really hard, but the heat was hard on her and the smell made her ill. I made her take breaks and rest, but even though she was "a tiny little thing" as Katrina called her, she hauled many loads to the curb.

On the second day while we were taking a break, a police cruiser drove up and wanted to talk to us. The 8th Ward was a pretty rough area and the police were driving military-type Hummers, so it was a little intimidating. The police officer stopped and asked, "Who's in charge?" I had been dubbed the "Gentle General," so that meant I was elected. I listened as the police told me a story that made all of us realize just how dangerous an area we were in.

Torry was standing next to me when the police officer explained that, a couple blocks over, a man had been murdered. He was changing a tire when someone rode up on a bike and shot him in the head. The police had no idea what the motive may have been, so it was possible that it was a random shooting. The policeman said, "We know the shooter is somewhere around here because he took off on foot, so we're pretty sure he is in one of these houses."

Todd and Torry talking to policeman in a Hummer

There were four facts I quickly considered: First, some-one had been murdered in cold blood. Second, all of the houses were vacant because they had to be gutted and re-built. Third, a killer was close by and he had a gun. And fourth, the policeman had just warned us to be careful and left. At that point it was clear that we were on our own, so I gathered everyone together and we stood right there in the street and prayed.

Afterwards, I felt at peace that we were there under God's protection. Everyone agreed that we wanted to complete the work. We dug in and finished the job by the end of the second day.

On our last day in New Orleans, we were scheduled to hand out supplies at a local church. Katrina and her husband had picked up a truckload of supplies earlier from a special warehouse in Georgia. Evidently supplies are stockpiled for emergencies and natural disasters, because the warehouse was filled with furniture, mattresses, bedding, diapers, cans of food, all types and sizes of clothes, and just about anything a person needed to set up basic housekeeping.

This was where Torry shined. She was working with people and helping them pick out the supplies they needed. At 13 years old, she loved to shop, so it was great to play "personal shopper," and the people of New Orleans seemed to enjoy her enthusiasm. Torry was too young to realize it, but she wasn't just helping 'customers' pick out clothes and furniture; she honored the people with respect by helping them.

When people think of the damage Katrina left behind, they think of images from the news, magazines and the web, but they can't feel the heat or smell the decay.

New Orleans, with its jazz music, spicy Creole cooking, and a culture rich with history and tradition, was now a corpse of its former self. In empathy, people from all over the country came together and gave their time and sweat to help resurrect that once great city.

Katrina Golden said, "God was all over this trip! Not many people get up and go one day to a place that had just suffered a devastating hurricane, a 'Storm of the Century' hurricane! Todd's doing things I want to do. If he listened to the naysayers, he wouldn't be doing what he is with Barnabas. I say, 'If God has put something on your heart, don't let

Torry, helping a woman select items for her family

outside influences make you give up what you have been called to do.'"

I've told Torry and Alex many times, "This is who we are. If you remember anything from me, remember that I love you and that we help other people. It is our responsibility."

Through my own journey I learned that talking isn't always the best way to teach. It's easy to get caught up and let the key point of the scripture get out of focus and do things so others will praise *us* when the focus should be on bringing glory to God. Scripture confirms this instruction in Matthew 5:16: *You should be a light for other people. Live so that they will see the good things you do and will praise your Father in Heaven.*

From left to right: Alex, Laura Hochberger, Torry, Todd, and Katrina Golden standing outside the Hochberger's house.

I am constantly reminded of the distinction between preaching to youth and teaching through personal example. Robert Shaffer says, "We must view young people not as empty bottles to be filled, but as candles to be lit."

My goal when working with youth in missions and with my own children is to show the love of Jesus through my actions because I believe that Jesus will fulfill their needs, whereas I am simply a vehicle charged to bring the Good News of Christ.

Action Faith

"Oh crap, I'm gonna get crushed!" was all I could think of in that moment when the man who would be my opponent stepped forward. He was a completely intimidating hulk of a man at 6'6, and probably 275 pounds. After several rounds of competition, it had gotten down to me and the hulk for the win. I knew the big guy could take me out with one good push, so the only chance I had to win for my team was to try and out-maneuver him; which is a nice way of saying that I planned to stay out of his way and hopefully avoid getting flattened.

I was attending a Christian leadership program and the competition was part of an exercise the teams participated in on our first night in Ecuador. They split the group into three teams and the exercise required a person from each team to volunteer to represent the other members of their group in a competition. If that person won, then the whole team would win. The exercise was to balance on one foot and knock the other person out of the circle; sort of like a one-footed wrestling match. I had volunteered to represent our team, which in hindsight was kind of foolish because I had undergone surgery for a torn ligament in my knee only two months earlier. But since I wasn't planning to jump on that leg I thought it would be fine. After all, this was just a Christian conference-type trip. Yeah, famous last words.

In the ring together, we backed up, dropped our shoulders and hit each other. I thought I'd just run into a brick wall, but by some miracle I didn't fall down and both of us were still standing. I could see the second pass was going to be different. We both backed up again and it was clear to everyone that the big guy was gearing up to come in with all his might and take me out.

Once again we dropped our shoulders, but I had a plan and just as the big guy lunged forward to smash into me, I hopped to the side. Since he didn't hit his target, the big Goliath had too much momentum going to stop and couldn't maintain his balance. He fell and I got the win for our team! It was a total God moment because the outcome fit perfectly with the lesson of the day about challenges faced by Christians who were leaders in business, as well as those serving on tight budgets in the mission field and faced by what seem like insurmountable odds.

I was participating in a program called Leader Mundial (pronounced, moon-de-al) after receiving an unexpected call from Russ Cline, founder of the Leader Mundial organization. Russ's dad is Ron Cline, the president of HCJB Radio and leader of the mission trip to South Africa that I had recently taken. Russ asked me to sponsor two missionaries from Africa and attend the conference myself. The timing was uncanny because it was only a month before I would be returning to South Africa for a three month trip in which I would be working directly with one of the missionaries I was sponsoring, Pierre Roux.

Leader Mundial was created in 2006 to bring together leaders from around the world and partner them with missionaries. The word *mundial* means "worldwide" in Spanish, making the name synonymous with its purpose of world-wide Christian leadership. What's extraordinary about this organization is that the program benefits people in the mission field as well as business leaders from all over the world who serve as sponsors. These reciprocal benefits are accomplished by having both groups attend the leadership program with a goal of developing ongoing relationships. An even more unpredictable event was how God brought me together with Pierre who would become a brother and spiritual mentor.

Pierre later shared some insights and identified areas that presented challenges for me as I began the transition from the secular world to the mission field.

As he described it later:

> I felt right away that Todd had a big heart. His first question to me after meeting was, "What do you need?" We got on from the start like a house on fire and participated in all of the same events at Leader Mundial because the model is to have Todd teach me business skills and for me to sew spirituality into his life.
>
> I remember that he was challenged when all the businessmen got together to talk about various models for raising money to fund their charities. Todd presented his ideas and three of the wealthiest men in the room shot down every one. But I watched him take their criticism without letting it extinguish his enthusiasm. God helped him persevere and to this day Barnabas continues to grow and serve, whereas the other three charities have struggled.
>
> In the years I've known Todd, it's been wonderful to see how his faith has grown. In the beginning, he would make decisions according to

Todd. Now he spends more time pursuing what God is telling him through the Bible.

His heart is invested in helping to make a difference in the lives of people. So it's going to be a challenge when the help Barnabas provides is used by men who will buy booze to get drunk and then beat their wives instead of making a better life for their families. It's going to be challenging when meaningful projects are derailed; particularly because projects involve support from those who want to see immediate results confirming that their support is making a difference.

I know Todd is aware that he is challenged by the need for patience. Like all of us, he wants everything finished tomorrow. I think he is frustrated when things are not taking off as quickly as he feels they should be. It's not easy, not when you are used to making things happen on your own. However, it's absolutely necessary for what he's going to go through next.

God is taking him through the grinder to have him experience different things because Satan is going to attack him and he has to be ready to handle it.

Pierre's criticism fires me up to improve because I know it comes from love. In some respects, my journey illustrates the normal stages of growth we go through as Christians and the choices we are given to determine what our faith will look like. A that movement is growing in churches is to have what is called 'action faith'. People are no longer waiting for a 'calling' to be bold in their faith by helping others in the name of Jesus. 'Action faith' is being embraced by youth around the world. More kids are going on mission trips now than ever before, both inside and outside of their countries. As parents and mentors, we can help by encouraging our children to grow up with the understanding that reaching out is essential to being Christian.

There's no particular stage a believer has to achieve before they are ready to be part of mission work. The belief that a person must be mature in their faith or have in-depth knowledge of the Bible before they can serve is simply untrue. It's so exciting for me to see kids go with others of their same age on a mission trip to a country like Mexico. But it doesn't have to be formal event. Adults and youth alike are serving in their communities by having a pop-can drive to raise money for the local food bank, or organizing a collection of shoes, coats, mittens, and hats to help kids who would otherwise go without.

The native philosopher, Teton Lakota advises, "Tell me and I will forget. Show me and I will learn. Involve me and I will understand." Everything we do matters to God. No matter what you do, if it's done out of love then you've chosen to put your faith into action.

Todd and Pierre at the Leader Mundial conference

Ninety Days of Grace

I was filled with anticipation as I neared the end of the flight to South Africa for my three month trip. It was a beautiful sunny day when I landed in Cape Town on March 24, 2007, the day after my daughter's birthday. It was difficult to be away from Torry on her birthday, but she made it easier for me by sending a sweet note saying, "I miss you, but I'm glad you are in Africa helping people and I can't wait to hear what you have been doing. Love you tons, Torry."

Pierre picked me up at the airport and helped me get settled into the Bed and Breakfast that would be my home for the next three months. It was located in a small town named Fish Hoek, about 20 minutes from Cape Town. The location was ideal because it was close to the ocean, just down the road from where Pierre and his family lived. During this trip I would primarily be working with Pierre and a representative from the Living Hope missionary organization, named Pat Ball.

The first morning, Pierre brought me down to the ocean where we had coffee and talked for hours about what I was hoping to accomplish during my stay. When we talked about transportation Pierre let me know that we would travel together and he would show me different projects so I could select ones that were a good fit for Barnabas. I had to laugh when he said that he owned a Toyota Camry which he said was an acronym for 'Christ And Me Reaching Youth.'" Working with young people was a passion we both shared.

Then, in the late afternoon Pat Ball picked me up and even let me drive her car. It happened to be my first time driving on what an American intuitively feels is the *wrong* side of the road. There are a lot of adjustments to make. For one, you have to work the gear shift of the car's manual transmission with the opposite hand. It's a bizarre feeling to see cars coming at you in the lane we're programmed to drive in from the time we get our license at sixteen years old. It felt like I was driving the wrong way on a one-way street.

Clearly, Pat had a lot of faith in me that day! At one point I pulled out of a parking spot and began driving on the right side of the road. Pat said in a conversational tone, "You might want to move to the other side of the road now, Todd." I let her drive the rest of the day.

One of the things Pat helped me with was putting an agenda together. She cautioned me to set aside ideas of a fixed schedule, explaining that her group is disciplined and works hard, but they don't force things to happen because there is never a shortage of work to do. She told me later that she could sense that I needed to follow God's plan here and let things happen according to His timetable.

I still felt I needed some sort of itinerary to feel comfortable because there were a number of things I wanted to be sure didn't fall through the cracks. So we developed a tentative schedule. That night I witnessed a magnificent sunset serving as a backdrop to huge waves that created a crescendo of sound as they crashed into the rocks. I sat in silence and just soaked in the raw beauty of the sight.

Things got busy the next day as I travelled to Masiphumelele (Masi) Baptist Church inside the township of Masiphumelele. One of the first people I met was the church's youth pastor, Sonwabo, who became a treasured friend. Sonwabo is the kind of man who laughs easily and smiles most of the time. He has an easy going, playful way about him that just sets people at ease. Coupled with passionate devotion to God that radiates warmth; he is an excellent example of Jesus' light shining through a Christian.

While talking to the interim pastor, named Deba, at Masi church, we discussed the horrible tragedy the church had been through a few months earlier and how the people were still in the process of healing. Their pastor, who I had met on my previous trip to South Africa, had been murdered at the church by an unstable man he had been counselling. The man had walked into the church and shot the pastor point blank. The bullet hole could still be seen in the walls of the church.

Deba asked if I would be willing to give the devotions on Monday and Tuesday at their Oceanview facility to help out, as he had assumed the role of pastor until a permanent replacement was found. I was honored and gladly accepted the opportunity. It wasn't on the agenda I had set with Pat Ball on the first day I arrived, but I could work it in with no problem.

Then later on the same day, Sonwabo told me that his dad had suffered a major heart attack and he needed to leave for a short time. He had heard from Deba that I agreed to do the devotions at Oceanview, so I was surprised for the second time that day when he asked if I would teach the lesson to the youth group at Masi on Tuesday nights. I was humbled and I just prayed they would be able to understand me because of the language barrier.

It didn't escape my notice that this was another commitment that affected the game plan I had established upon arriving in South Africa. I thought, "Hmmm. Maybe there was something to Pat's advice to me that there's always plenty of work to do and that God will set my agenda." At that moment I started to understand and loosened the grip on my plan. There were still things I really wanted to do on this trip, but I wasn't going to get stressed if God decided he wanted me to do something else.

The need to shift plans happened again five days after arriving, when I had the good fortune of joining Pierre, my first contact in Africa, to meet up with Jerry Carnill and his team to look at new ministry opportunities. It was a enormous blessing to work alongside this experienced group of people from the mission field.

Our first stop was Barcelona Orphanage, located outside the city of Cape Town. When we walked into the orphanage and saw the precious children, I was overwhelmed with a desire to help improve their lives. As in other third-world countries, many children are orphaned because of parents with AIDS or even simple injuries that go untreated or become infected. With the shortage of medicine, a bacterial illness or injury can be life threatening. Some children are simply abandoned.

I was told there used to be a sign as you entered the orphanage that read, "Enter at your own risk." Now the sign is gone because it was used for the side of a house. The need is so great it's almost unbearable. This small orphanage currently has 14 children, 10 of whom are infected with HIV. It was hard not to leave with one of the precious children in my arms.

I had been playing with an adorably happy little boy who couldn't have been more than two years old. I was told he had been rescued after being abandoned. The little boy with big brown eyes was found inside a dumpster wrapped in a plastic bag. He had been crying, probably screaming in terror, when someone heard him and pulled him out of the dumpster, saving his life.

It was horrifying to fathom a mother throwing away her baby like garbage, but I learned it happened more than I wanted to know. It was a heartbreaking reality of life just miles outside the surprisingly modern city of Cape Town.

Todd, holding the little boy who was rescued from a dumpster

After leaving the orphanage, we went to Woodstock Baptist Church. I was excited to learn about what I'd heard the church was doing to help the unemployed find work and teach life skills classes. The programs were highly success-ful and it was amazing to see and hear some of the stories, especially because job creation was a strong interest of mine. The Chinese proverb still holds true: "Give a man a fish and you feed him for a day. Teach a man to fish and you feed him for a lifetime." I was completely amazed by what these people were accomplishing with surprisingly little fund-ing to work with.

The next deviation from my plan came by way of a dev-astating shock that turned my world upside-down with one phone call. I had settled into my three month stay in South Africa. It took a little while to become accustomed to the dif-ferent pace of life there, but I loved it. I had brought my bike along and got into a habit of riding 30 or so miles every day. I felt so alive! I was in shape and the improvement in my health allowed me to reduce my insulin injections to just one a day for the first time since my diagnosis in High School.

I also felt I was finally coming to terms with the inescap-able end of my marriage. As far as anyone could see, I had accepted the divorce, perhaps not at peace about it but at least more accepting. I had learned that a smile can be an effective disguise.

It was a beautiful Saturday morning and I was on my way out for a bike ride. A friend of mine was at home and she and I were planning to meet up later in the day. She has an amazingly nurturing soul along with an encouraging spirit and we became good friends during my three month stay in South Africa. It's amazing to me how God places the right people in our paths to help us find our way when we feel lost.

She remembered the next moments with sadness:

It was mid-morning when I heard my gate bell ring. It was Todd. I went out to my gate to let him in and I knew something was really wrong. Todd walked in and just sat down; he looked devastated. I said, "I thought you were riding?" He didn't look up as he replied, "No, we need to talk."

He had just received the news from his lawyer that his ex-wife was selling the company he had founded! Worse still, he found out she had been planning it for over a year.

His wife had agreed that Todd would run Barnabas Charities full time while she ran GB Synergy for him; but it had been a deception from the beginning. She had maneuvered her strategy for money and prestige. Every detail, including the timing, was orchestrated, and the last step was happening while he was on the other side of the world. It was a complete betrayal.

I couldn't wrap my head around the news that my wife had been planning it for so long. My lawyer said she was selling GB Synergy to a company out of Charlotte, NC. I was in a near panic trying to fax and email and call all at once to get information. Having the woman you love divorce you out of the blue is devastating, but to discover that she had been planning the take-over of your company for over a year, and coming to the cold realization that you had been manipulated by someone you trusted beyond measure left an indelible mark on my heart.

My friend prayed for me on the spot. She later said, "Todd is usually so resilient, but I was worried about him personally; he was so devastated. I've never seen him like that before or since."

My downward spiral continued as I began thinking of all the things we did together over the past year with our church and personally as a couple. It was beyond comprehension how I could have been so fooled. It was sickening to think about how I had been so in love and trusting that I handed her my company and my livelihood on a silver platter.

Mark and Diane Beede later shared their thoughts:

> There was a time we were really worried about Todd. We think what saved him was being involved with Barnabas and putting his passion back into serving the Lord even deeper than he did before. Instead of going for the business success, he wanted to point his life in a totally different direction. For Todd these were not just words. He cares about the people, and about God and about doing the right thing. To my knowledge that's what he has done ever since.

> He lost GB Synergy, lost the majority of his finances and through it found a higher calling. It was pretty amazing. Once the shock of it was over you could tell that he had found a whole new level of fulfillment that he didn't even know existed.

My friends probably gave me more credit than I deserved because I was in survival-mode and had nothing to hold on to except my faith in God. I believe God gave me a purpose greater than my own troubles and it's what held me together. Pierre and Pat kept me in the Word and I clung to God's promise to us in Isaiah 43:2-3: *When you go through the deep waters, I will be with you. When you go through rivers of difficulty, you will not drown. When you walk through the fire of oppression, you will not be burned up; the flames will not consume you; for I am the Lord, your God.*

I took the advice of my friends and slowed the pace a little and took time to spend alone with God. In one week I had ridden over 200 miles through the mountains. My decision centered me so I could focus on what God had brought me here to do. I hadn't come this far to fail.

The following Sunday service at the church in Masiphumelele was intensely spirit-filled and lifted me up like no other service I'd ever experienced. After collecting the offering, the congregation started singing and dancing down the aisles. The preacher would start talking, then someone would stand up, start singing and the entire congregation would pick up the song and start singing with them. My eyebrows shot up in surprise when the spontaneous disruption of the service occurred, then a smile grew that stretched from ear to ear as I watched the scene unfold. It was awesome and before I could think twice I was up dancing and trying to sing along with them. This went on for the whole service. It took a long time for the pastor to get all the way through his message, but he didn't seem to mind in the least and the presence of the Holy Spirit was undeniable! I needed this intense spiritual lift.

Clearly God wanted me to get out of the pew and witness the Holy Spirit in a totally new way. There was so much joy. They lived in conditions that Americans would consider impoverished, and yet these South African people were filled with thankfulness for God's abundant love. We Americans could learn a lot from them. Some may say, "This is the life they've always lived, they don't have anything to compare it to like we do." To that the response should be, "How lucky they are to have so little that they sing up and down the aisles thanking God and depending on the Lord for everything they need; they redefine the meaning of *wealth*."

After speaking about forgiveness on Monday night at Oceanview, I was fired up to lead devotions for the Tuesday night 18 to 25 year old group. I try to use my own experiences and the lessons I've learned from them in my message. That night I was speaking about having Jesus take your pain, worries or loneliness. The kids connected with the message, but I also gained healing from giving the message. That's how God works sometimes and why we have to just follow His lead.

A dear friend was with me that night and remembered this time as a period of spiritual growth:

> I've been proud of Todd many times, but one that sticks out is when he was working with the Youth in the Bible Studies. He tried so hard to help them understand that Jesus was the one who could fill the void in their lives.
>
> Their lives are so difficult by anyone's standards. They don't have money, many don't have homes, and the ones that do have homes are generally referring to a cardboard shelter. And they are facing futures that are not all that hopeful. I really think when he was there in the Bible Study with those kids, he was truly walking in the footsteps of Barnabas, The Encourager, teaching them that Jesus can fill that hole in their heart and He can guide them to those things of value instead of turning to drugs, alcohol and sex.

There were times when it wasn't easy or comfortable to live this way. I remember one day we went to help at the sports camps and I had an experience that really made me think about what I'm doing and how I have been acting.

I had been asking God to help me be open and loving to people. Since the situation with my ex-wife, I noticed myself pulling away and I didn't want to become that person. I wanted to keep moving forward, even if it was just in baby steps and I didn't want to hold back when it came to loving people. So, I grabbed a hold of the newly popular WWJD "What would Jesus Do" saying and put it to use. I tried to pass situations through a filter of "How would Jesus want me to act if he were here?"

Then it happened. I was tested when I saw a baby all alone, he couldn't have been more than a year or two old. I walked over to where he was sitting and after he warmed up to me I picked him up. As soon as I picked up the baby I realized there was an odor and wetness coming from him that was something I'd never experienced before in my life. My thoughts went immediately to my recent prayers and I thought of showing this child love no matter what.

I brought him over to someone who could wash him up and as I was walking away I realized there was urine and excrement on my shirt, arms, legs; it was all over me. The odor hit me and I literally had to force myself not to vomit. It was the worst smell I've ever known in my life and even after changing my clothes and having a good scrubbing in an extra long shower I could still smell it.

The moral of this story isn't to test your resolve by finding the stinkiest kid to hang out with all day. The lesson is simply that, when we dedicate our lives to serving the Lord, there will be things we must do that are not going to be pleasant, but there cannot be a distinction in who we love. To walk like Jesus, to talk like Jesus, we must force ourselves sometimes to put our own comfort on a shelf because our action or inaction reflects directly on Jesus' reputation. It was remarkable how much I had experienced and grown during the first month of my trip.

My second month in Africa was a cram session in faith, healing, giving and growth as lesson after lesson brought me closer to the Lord. It started with a majestic sunrise service on Easter morning. While the congregation was gathered on the beach in Fish Hoek celebrating Jesus' resurrection, I noticed a man out of the corner of my eye walking alone by the shore. The man was clearly homeless and I felt a push to reach out to this stranger on the beach; but I didn't do anything. We were in the middle of a service and the man hadn't looked my way to notice that I had seen him. I hesitated too long and the man was gone. Every Easter I think about that man and how I failed to reach out. If I had only called out or walked over to the man, if I had invited him to worship and fed him a warm meal who knows what kind of impact it may have made. If nothing else, the man would have had fellowship and a full belly.

The enemy will try to cement our feet, but love must conquer even when it's awkward. Regret comes from letting something of importance go by us. The "if only I..." and "I wish I..." statements are universal in their meaning. Through Jesus, God taught us that His love is not passive and by that example ours shouldn't be either.

We can see this truth in James 2:22-24:

> You see that his faith and his actions were working together, and his faith was made complete by what he did. And the scripture was fulfilled

that says, "Abraham believed God, and it was credited to him as righteousness, and he was called God's friend." You see that a person is considered righteous by what they do and not by faith alone.

God pushed me forward in my faith once again when I was given the opportunity to deliver the Sunday morning message at Woodstock Baptist Church in Cape Town. Man, I was so nervous! But it turned out to be one of the greatest gifts I received while in South Africa. I'm not a minister and I've never been to seminary or had any formal training and here I was being tapped to give a message on Sunday morning. As nervous as I was, I was excited at the same time. Pierre helped me with scripture to illustrate how God's promise will provide all we need. None of us walk through this life alone so I was thankful for his guidance in helping me prepare. Pierre shared his thought saying:

> He doesn't know the Bible as a pastor would, but I think the lesson for Todd was that in mission work a person doesn't need to have formal training in order to be effective. Public speaking is a gift that comes naturally for him and people are engaged because he talks as if he's conversing with an old friend instead of 'preaching.' A lot of times there is a language barrier, but that doesn't seem to hinder getting his message across.

My message was that in order to receive complete healing we need to do three things: First, we need to make a decision that we want to be healed. Second, we must have faith that God can heal us. And third, we must go toward

God to be healed. The key was to acknowledge that faith is not passive; it requires action on our part.

Talking to the congregation that morning helped me grow. I had to humble myself and share some experiences that had left a metaphorical hole in my own heart. I felt the Holy Spirit was speaking through me, or maybe even to me, but it was a message I felt passionate about, so I was elated when the congregation responded positively.

Beaufort West

It's hard to believe someone living off what they can scavenge in a city dump could be thankful. The dump is riddled with filth, abuse and disease, but the people are faithful and thankful, yes *thankful,* for what they have. Pierre and I both have a calling for the people living in the city dumps of Beaufort West because it's a huge challenge. Pierre explains:

The children are the sweetest things you've ever seen. I love the spirit of the women in Beaufort West. Most of the people who are active are the ladies and they are passionate about what they do, but they don't get any support. In fact there are more illegal alcohol stores than anything else. They try to be Biblical women in a non-biblical area and it is not easy. I love to see how, in spite of the odds, they have such a passion to help the children create a better life.

While there is an abundance of good in many of the people, there is also evil that surrounds this area. A main focus of the women who are making a difference is to guide the boys and girls in sexual matters. There is a massive problem with sexual promiscuity and prostitution with the young girls and boys. The children live in tiny houses with their mother and father, so they see everything that goes on and then they go out and imitate it.

The education of the children has to begin at a very young age to have a chance at making a difference. Even then, it frequently isn't effective because of the impoverished state the people live in. There is no money, so the South African government, not unlike Welfare in the United States, gives a grant to unwed mothers.

The women think they can have a baby and get money for clothing, make-up, etcetera. The reality is that the money isn't enough to take care of even the one baby. So, they have a second baby thinking it will take care of their money shortage, but it doesn't. And so on it goes, around and around in a vicious cycle.

A shack that serves as a home in Beaufort West

A child carried by her brother in Beaufort West dump

When the most abundant stores in the area are illegal liquor stores, it's not surprising that alcoholism is the main factor in the abuse of women and children. It would seem no one could afford alcohol, but we know that is not true. Where there is a desire, there is a way to fulfill it. We have been so exposed to this fact that many of us have become desensitized. Perhaps God felt I needed an emotional wake-up call so I could be affected and, if that was His plan, then it worked! With a combination of disgust, compassion, frustration, and sadness, Pierre explains:

> The men drink this incredibly cheap rubbish that makes them blind. They drink until they are drunk and then go beat their wives. We see many women sleeping under the bridge with their little children. That's why there are so many street children in Beaufort West. It's one of the

few areas where people have homes to go to, but because of the threat of a beating or rape, the children prefer to live on the streets.

Road sign at the entrance to Beaufort West.
"Hands off our children. Sex with children is a crime.
2 out of 7 are affected by sexual abuse."

A native of Zambia, Pierre found his home in South Africa. As the man on the ground, he is the first point of contact for several organizations and consequently wears a lot of different hats. Pierre works primarily with short term mission teams. He facilitates and arranges the teams from overseas by setting their itinerary, accommodations, and transport. Many of the teams do work in South Africa but they do not have experience with either the people or customs, so Pierre is invaluable as someone who can help them along the way. Pierre once told me, "I believe in building God's Kingdom, not my own empire, so I will help in any way I can if it is the will of God."

My work is a little different. I'll ask Pierre about a project and he will research it and give me his advice. He knows what he's doing over there and I value his experience as well as his friendship. Pierre takes me to see the projects and once we've identified a good match, I go about raising awareness and securing funding for the projects through Barnabas Charities. It is a partnership that has resulted in facilitating some good results for the people of Africa.

While I had made good strides, there was an area my mentors unanimously agreed that I needed to work on and that was Bible study. It seemed everyone had suggestions, but I felt strongly that a person didn't have to know the Bible intimately in order to serve and make a difference. And there was truth to my logic because people are needed at all stages of their walk with Christ. Pierre told me, "That is true to a degree, but I stand in agreement with Ron Cline and Jerry Carnill that you need to get into the Word of God. And I think you are beginning to do that now."

It was a slow start for me. I wanted to dedicate my life to the Lord and do good works, but I wasn't passionate about reading the Bible. I had never spent a lot of time in the Word and I wasn't filled with the 'hunger' I'd heard other Christians talk about. It is one thing to flip through the Bible on Sunday morning to keep up with the passages the pastor is reading, but it's entirely another to study those passages.

The difference comes down to reading versus learning. In order to be credible in the mission field it is critical to understand the lessons taught in the Bible, so God's word is behind your message and actions. But how does one go about getting into the word without a lifetime history of regularly reading the Bible, or without having been to Seminary? Pierre explained exactly how it is accomplished with a patient smile in his voice:

Oh, it's so easy. God doesn't want everyone
to go to the Seminary. All of us are called to be

missionaries in one form or another. Wherever we are is a mission field. Todd will have to put the extra effort in to developing that relationship with God. But whether it's in the business field trying to create jobs, or helping people in missions, his business forté can help the small organizations that we have here in South Africa and in the rest of the world. For example, he can teach someone in one of these organizations how to set up simple accounting books and how to run those books with integrity. It's the intent behind the action that shows the love of Jesus.

People get confused thinking that the reason it is important to study the Bible is so you can preach, but you study to *understand*. Jesus didn't just preach, he went around door to door and travelled. He took the Gospel one step at a time. And he showed his love to the people. That's what he's calling us to do. It's not just words. It's not to just stand up and preach. It's to show the love of Jesus by what you do.

A great example is of a simple missionary who went to a foreign country to work with a missionary organization, but the organization wouldn't let him in because he didn't speak the native language. Eventually he became frustrated and went to the 'mission country' anyway and became a servant, working hand in hand there with the people. Many years later a missionary group came in and started speaking about Jesus, and the people looked around and said, "But we had that man living with us for 5 years."

God is calling us to emulate Jesus. The Holy Spirit will give you the words to say, but obviously you need to put in the time as well. Jesus taught the disciples personally. In the same way the Holy Spirit teaches us personally and the more time you spend in the Word, the more you will learn. And the more Todd gets into the mission field the more time he will need to spend in the Word, not less, so that he is ready to give an answer. Getting into the word of God allows you to be impactful. It helps to be around people who make reading the Bible part of their day, so when we travel it's a great time for Todd and me to worship together.

I believe he will have the desire to do so. Satan likes to rob us of our joy and hunger for the Word. My personal philosophy for anyone starting to get into the Bible is to start in the book of John. I also like to read a Proverb every day. There are 31, so there is a Proverb for every day of the month. I try to read a Psalm every day; one Old Testament chapter, and one New Testament chapter. The chapters are really short and if you read 4 chapters in the Bible a day, you will have read it in a year!

Pierre always tells me the truth, whether it's what I want to hear or need to hear. It is a journey and I have a lot to learn along the way. But we are capable of learning *as* we serve; they are not mutually exclusive. One thing I've learned is that making an impact happens when others can relate to you and being relatable is nothing more than having life experiences. People want to learn from others who have been there and done that. It's very hard to go and witness to someone who has an addiction if you haven't seen trauma in your own life. That doesn't mean you have to be an alcoholic to understand the damage alcohol can do. There are many things other than alcohol that are addictions, such as sex, money, work, gambling, eating, and so on.

For every challenging moment in the field, there are a hundred others that make it all worthwhile. One of those moments happened when Pierre and I travelled through the Northern Cape.

There was a project Pierre wanted me to see and to get there we had to drive through the mountains of Springbok. This area of the Northern Cape is called the "Karoo" and is known for being a nearly lifeless scrubland in the summer, then transforming itself into an explosion of color when the winter rains wake up the dormant flowers. As we drove out of Springbok into the wide open spaces of the Karoo, there were no people, no houses, no animals, just a whole lot of nothing for miles and miles.

After awhile we came upon a normal looking outcropping of rocks with the words "Tourist Attraction" painted on a large boulder. I barked a single laugh at the sarcastic sign and looked over to Pierre expecting to see him smirking as well. But he had a thoughtful look on his face as he pointed and told me to pull over the car. I looked at him thinking, "Are you serious?" But I did as he asked and stepped out. Pierre didn't give me any explanation as he got out and walked over to the rocks where we both sat down. At first I was confused about why we were there and then a startled look must have come over my face because Pierre finally smiled.

I broke the silence saying, "Hey, do you hear that?"

"Hear what?" Pierre said with a knowing smile.

"Nothing," I said, "there's no sound. No animals, no birds, no wind…nothing!"

It was deafeningly quiet; almost scary. I call it the quietest place on earth. Pierre explained, "There is no sound on a day like this when there is no wind. The Karoo can be like that especially when you can see that the grass is not blowing and there are no animal tracks in the sand. It is a profound moment when you experience the power of silence."

The road through the Karoo

Khayelitsha and Zimbabwe

The South African township of Khayelitsha was created while the country was still under the apartheid regime to control the 'problem' of the growing black population. People were forcefully relocated to Khayelitsha in a system called "Influx Control." With little or no financial assistance from their government, most built shacks made from tin, wood, or cardboard.

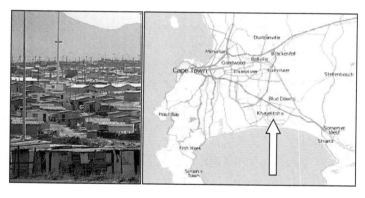

Left: Shacks in Khayelitsha
Right: Map showing Khayelitsha near Cape Town

As you might imagine, some of the relocations were far from peaceful because our human nature resists being forced to do things deemed by other to be 'good for us'. Perhaps that's one reason God makes our salvation a *choice*. We must choose to give our lives freely to the Lord, to be reborn again by accepting Jesus as our Savior.

Although Apartheid was officially abolished in 1990, the first election won by a black African, Nelson Mandela, was in 1994, and unofficial Apartheid was still felt by people like the residents of Khayelitsha. They certainly were not receiving government support for development and improvement of their living conditions.

Ironically, Khayelitsha is the fastest growing township in South Africa, with 406,779 residents as of the 2005 census. Seven years later, the population has significantly increased. Yet the money still belongs to the mostly white population in the Western Cape, who are also largely the people who vote.[9]

That political disadvantage leaves half a million people in virtual bondage. Oppression causes hopeless depression in some, rebellious rage in others, and at times results in a defiant disregard of the law created by a government who they feel has all but ignored their existence.[10] This turmoil can create a dangerous situation for well-meaning white missionaries.

Fortunately Barnabas, Living Hope, ATAIM, and other travellers coming to this area on mission trips have Pierre Roux. As a Colonel in the Army, he is more than capable of keeping the guests of his country safe. Potential mischief makers don't mess with his teams because they know and respect him as an honest man of integrity who is committed to helping them. They also know under the velvet glove is a steel fist.

The most arresting statistic of this huge community is not that the ratio of the population is 99% black to 1% white; it's the *age* of the population. Only 7% of the half million people living in Khayelitsha are over 50 years old. Having 93% of the population under 50 is unimaginable for people living in the United States, but even more heartbreaking is that over 200,000 people are under 19 years old.[11] In our culture, at 19, you are barely an adult. It's not surprising that there are many orphans and street children. Some are orphans because their parents are no longer alive; others prefer to live on the streets rather than be abused at home; and still others were callously abandoned.

The good news is that approximately 75% of the residents consider themselves to be Christians. So a massive opportunity exists to make a difference in the lives of the people of Khayelitsha. They need Jesus because His love is powerful enough to interrupt the continuous circle of hopelessness.

One of the first times I visited Khayelitsha, I met a 50-something woman named Mimi who ran a Bed and Breakfast in town. She noticed that the children weren't doing well in school and thought it might be because they weren't getting proper nutrition, so she started a ministry called, "Mimi's Soup Kitchen."

Mimi began feeding sixty school age children one meal every day before school, which was the only meal some of them would have all day. Her dream was to run the soup kitchen full-time and cook two meals a day for the children, but that would mean she would have to leave her job. Mimi had to work in order to make enough money to support herself and buy the food to feed the children.

After returning to Fish Hoek, I reached out by way of the Barnabas Charities blog, asking for a group or an individual who would support Mimi's Soup Kitchen. It would take $500 per month to lift the project to the next level. Within a very short time. a couple from Denver responded with a commitment to support Mimi's Soup Kitchen for the next 12 months.

That couple has sponsored the project ever since, allowing Mimi to achieve her dream of working full-time at the soup kitchen. She exceeded her original goal by providing an astonishing two meals a day, one before school and one after school, for approximately 300 children! God blessed her and all of us by her example. It just goes to show there's no such thing as dreaming "too big!"

With admiration in his voice, Pierre said, "Mimi is very involved in her church and has high morals. She runs a bed & breakfast from her house so she always has someone staying there with her. The children adore her! We do the shopping for her with money provided by Barnabus Charities, held in a trust. Then we bring the food and supplies to her soup kitchen in Khayelitsha."

He explained the importance of having a trust fund for the projects:

> Every dollar of the money donated goes into a trust and is then allocated to projects. Every penny is accounted for. It's important to have these kinds of controls because the trust is audited by the government and by outside accountants and we have to produce a full report on every cent that has been donated. There are huge controls and integrity has made us become more and more popular.

The accountability is there for all to see. That kind of painstaking accountability isn't there for all charity organizations and it gives credibility.

The credibility of Barnabas Charities is critically important to me. I'm fortunate to have a partner like Pierre who is experienced in working with different charity and humanitarian organizations to keep strict controls over the money that has been provided for projects. After the victory of finding someone to sponsor the work Mimi was doing in Khayelitsha, I couldn't wait to travel to Zimbabwe and Malawi, the last two countries I would visit during this trip.

Zimbabwe was a different world than I had experienced up to this point in my South African adventure. The country was occupied by indigenous tribes and I felt an element of danger that I hadn't witnessed before. That reality was influenced by widespread corruption within the government and extreme economic instability. I learned a great deal about suffering, oppression, and abuse of humanity—and I also witnessed joy in spite of the terrible conditions. I have so much respect for their courageously strong spirits.

My education started right away when I learned that, like Khayelitsha, 99% of the Zimbabwe's population is black. President Robert Mugabe is also black, yet many black people are not able to exercise their voting rights. Their human rights are violated and freedom of the press is suppressed by the Zimbabwean government.[12] It doesn't take a rocket scientist to finish the equation and realize that 1% of the country's population controls the money and power.

Even more disturbing is that Zimbabwe is a major location for human sex trafficking, and the problem is worsening with the decline of their economy. Men, women, boys and girls are also 'harvested' from this land for forced labor, and the country is a thoroughfare for exporting people like a commodity from one country to another.

Zimbabwean law prohibits trafficking for sexual exploitation, but not all forms of human trafficking are prohibited. Prosecution is rare, because of the lack of a strong formal government.[13] Zimbabwe is a fertile hunting ground for predators. It was a horrifying reality.

A missionary named Gerald picked me up from the airport when I landed in Zimbabwe. He had a great sense of humor and we hit it off right away. I listened and took in my new surroundings as he talked about his ministry. Before long we wanted to stop and get some lunch so I asked Gerald if he knew of a bank where I could exchange my United States currency. When he took me to a nearby bank, I experienced the economic instability first hand. The bank's rate of exchange was $250 Zen to $1 US dollar. I was about to give the banker my money when Gerald stopped me saying he knew how to get me a better rate of exchange.

Gerald made a call and was told where to meet a man who would exchange my money into local currency. As we were driving down the street, we saw a group of men standing on the corner. Gerald was on the phone with his contact, who instructed us to pass by the group, continue on for another 200 meters and then park on the side of the street and await further instruction. It began to feel like a sketchy transaction was about to happen.

Fifteen minutes passed before Gerald's phone rang again and we received final instructions from the man. By this time I felt like we were in a movie on a covert operation; it felt surreal. The man told Gerald that we were to meet him behind the building where we were parked. What happened next was truly the stuff of movies.

Gerald gave him my 400 US dollars and the man gave me six million Zen dollars in exchange. Yes, that is right; I became a Zimbabwean multi-millionaire in one minute! The problem was that it cost us 126,000 Zen for a meal. So, being a millionaire was really a matter of perspective. Zimbabwe was experiencing unimaginable inflation. I experienced it again when I went to buy milk and the price had risen 50% overnight. Their economic system is in total chaos.

The next morning Gerald and I left at the crack of dawn for Victoria Falls. It was an 800 kilometer trek to our destination, a distance more challenging than I had predicted. I was definitely out of my element.

I found it more than a little disconcerting when we passed through a total of nine roadblocks complete with military guards who were armed with semi-automatic weapons.

We were pulled over and questioned at one point when the guards wanted to confirm the contents of my luggage and asked me to provide proof of my identity. While the guards were searching our car with their automatic guns slung over their shoulders, I couldn't help thinking about how they could shoot us right where we were standing, and no one would ever know exactly what had happened.

After we passed the last roadblock, I breathed easily for the first time in about twenty minutes.

Next, we pulled into a town looking for gas after noticing our tank was getting low, but none was available. People at the stations said that they had been out of gas for nearly three weeks! We decided that we had enough to make it to the next town, so we kept going. After trying in four more towns, we finally found a gas station that actually had gas but lacked the electricity to pump it into the car!

While we were talking to the people at the gas station, we noticed a man across the street waving at us. We walked over to talk and he said he had gasoline that we could buy. We followed him around the corner and into a hidden space behind the building where he had 20 liter plastic jugs of gas in the back of his pick-up truck. The price was 38,000 Zen per liter, so we paid the man an astronomical sum of 760,000 Zen for a jug of gas. So much for being a millionaire!

We were discussing the country and its ministry needs when all of a sudden the car shut down. We guided the car to the side of the road and sat for a minute before trying to start it up again. We turned the key and sure enough the car grumbled a bit, but it started. It seemed okay, so we continued on our way. After another 3 kilometers or so, it died again. This continued for what seemed like another 100 times until we finally reached our destination at Victoria Falls.

Each time the car sputtered out, we didn't know if it would start again. It turned out that the gas tank had dirt in it that caused filter problems. Finding a mechanic who would help us was also a problem. We kept getting referred to other people until we found a man who would help. He was located out of the way—but he turned out to be a great mechanic who fixed our car in no time.

Zimbabwe is in desperate times. It is hard for Americans to imagine not having electricity, water, gas, or food at any given time. I pray that this country can get its economy turned around. Part of the economic turmoil is based in the fact that, when the government needs more money, they just print more. They also use the black market for everyday exchanges.

It was increasingly clear to me that missionaries like Gerald were desperately needed in this place. He showed me several projects that would be good for Barnabas to take on, which allowed us to make a difference in a country with such great need. I wasn't discouraged because I truly believe a lot of small projects have the potential to make a big change.

A Leap of Faith

We stayed in Victoria Falls for two nights. In 1855, a Scottish missionary and doctor named David Livingstone renamed the falls "Victoria" after his Queen, but the site was originally called, "Mosi-oa-Tunya," which literally means the "Smoke that Thunders."[14] As the name implies, a spray is created when the water crashes into a basin of water at the bottom of the falls, creating what looks like inverted rain. The spray shoots at a height that can exceed 2,000 feet during the rainy season, and can be seen as far as 30 miles away.[15]

The falls were carved by the waters of the Zambezi River in a fracture of the earth over 5,600 feet in width! No mountains or deep valleys were involved in that creation. The falls are located in the midst of the basalt plateau, a flat land with a gash in the middle creating a majestic fall of a single sheet of water. It is bizarre and beautiful all at once.

After touring the falls, we walked over the Victoria Falls Bridge, which connects Zimbabwe with Zambia. Half way across the bridge we stopped at a place that offered bungee jumping and advertised itself as the 2nd longest bungee jump in the world. The jump is a free fall of approximately 350 feet into the Second Gorge over the Zambezi River.[16]

After watching people bungee jump for awhile, I thought it would be a great opportunity to make the jump as a symbolic "leap of faith." I like to say, "We must be willing to take risks in life in order to fully live." So I decided to walk the talk and registered for the jump.

Ironically, after I finally got up the nerve to register we were told to come back in an hour because it was the worker's lunch time. I thought, "Great. I get the nerve to bungee jump and they decide it's time to have lunch? Ugh!" I told Gerald that it must be a sign that I shouldn't make the jump, so we left and went to lunch. As we sat and talked, I changed my mind, deciding to put aside my fear and make the jump after all. I didn't want to look back on this day and regret my decision.

I'll admit I was terrified! As I stood on the bridge and looked down into the yawning gorge, I could just see the thin ribbon of blue that I was told was the Zambezi River. I was also reluctant because I had undergone surgery for a torn knee ligament just four months earlier. It was definitely risky to take a 350 foot free fall that included being jerked back up at the end of the descent by restraints secured around my ankles. But I pushed my fear aside as I sat down to have them attach the harness.

Three parts of the jump were scary. The first happened the second after I jumped off the platform and realized I had passed the point of no return. My inner voice was saying, "Uh oh! What did I just do? I'm gonna die." The adrenaline rush was like an injection right into my heart.

The seven second free fall felt like I was in slow motion. Then the second scary part happened when it struck me that the river was getting really close, really fast. I think I screamed, or at least I wanted to, even if it didn't actually come out of my mouth. I heard the noise of the rushing water in the distance from the falls and I could clearly see river and the intimidating rocks below. It seemed like I was going too fast to be able to stop in time

Todd bungee jumping at Victoria Falls over the Zambezi River

Then, WHOOSH, just before I would have hit the water, too close for comfort for sure, the cord tightened and I found myself bouncing back up so high that I actually flew under the bridge and came back up on the other side of it. Imagine my relief, followed by fear on the way back up as I saw the steel beams of the bridge getting closer at an alarming rate.

It's amazing how many things you can be consciously afraid of during just a few seconds. I was suspended in air for a moment, then another free fall. This time I wasn't scared about hitting the water, but I was still a little worried about the bridge, knowing I wasn't going to bounce back up as high this time. Then another whoosh, and back up I went.

After a few more yo-yos up and down, I was ready to be finished. The third scary part started when it felt like the straps on my ankles were shifting and would slip off my feet. They couldn't actually slip off, but it felt like it, nonetheless.

I sat upside down for another few minutes, which seemed like hours, before a man repelled down to me on a rope and secured me to his harness. They hoisted us back up to the bridge and, just like that, the experience was over.

It was such a rush!

Isn't this what life is about? Doesn't God want us all to take risks? Sometimes trusting God is about taking a metaphorical free fall on faith alone, knowing that, even when we are most afraid, God will be there to catch us.

Malawi

I expected the village children to be excited when they met me, as I had experienced in the past. But for the first time in Africa, the youth were not very friendly. In fact, they moved away from me and didn't like it when I took their picture or tried to show them the pictures. Most children in rural African have never seen a photograph of themselves or anyone else. Usually the kids are super excited and I can't snap the pictures quickly enough, but not here. After a long while, they warmed up a bit, having concluded that I was not a threat.

I was travelling with Petro, the youth pastor of Kindle Orphan Outreach, to a village east of the orphanage. He helped me understand the children's distrust, explaining that witchcraft was practiced by a tribe in the region that took children and killed them for certain body parts and discarded the rest of the corpse. The other threat was from outsiders who took children for slave and sex trade.

Ironically nicknamed "The warm heart of Africa," Malawi is indeed beautiful, but also frightening once I got a chance to look under its hood. I had arrived on a Friday and was given an excellent tour around the capital city of Lilongwe. After the tour, we drove to Kindle Orphan Outreach where I met Andrew and Francois Barr, the missionaries who ran the orphanage.

Saturday morning, Andrew and I, along with all of the kids, left for camping at Lake Malawi where his Church was spending the weekend. Lake Malawi is home to crocodiles and hippopotamuses, so I couldn't believe that people actually swam in it! Andrew explained that it was safe because the animals stay away from humans.

All I knew was that hippos were herbivores that appear to be gentle giants; but if they feel threatened, they will chomp you in half before you can finish saying "Help!" The crocs will roll you and take you to the bottom of the lake until you drown; then they tear you apart. Either way, it's pretty unsettling. They did convince me to join them but I had my eyes open whenever I swam underwater.

Todd (center, back row) with one of the Malawi youth groups he visited

Baboons and monkeys were everywhere—in the trees, and climbing the walls. The baboons, in particular, were always looking for a way to swoop in and steal our food.

During the night, I was assigned to sleep in a tent by an outer wall. We all retired to our tents and I was just dozing off when I heard noises and realized something was jumping off the walls into the area where we were sleeping.

A light was kept on at night in the camp to ward off animals, but apparently it didn't work very well, because the next thing I saw was the large shadows of baboons walking upright in a straight line outside of my tent. It was weird, but also made me bubble up inside with laughter. I think it seemed comical because they looked like monkey soldiers marching in a line. I learned later that baboons are the Malawian equivalent to our raccoons at a campsite, except they can be very dangerous.

Lake Malawi in East Africa: one of the world's great lakes

Eventually I fell asleep, only to be woken up in the middle of the night when I was attacked by thousands of ants! They were everywhere. After that, everyone in the camp was awake because apparently we had set up camp on a massive ant hill. It wasn't the most fun camping I've done, but it was definitely the most unique.

On Sunday, we attended a huge church service that was an amazing experience, beyond the powerful message delivered. Thirty-six countries were represented in the congregation. They all spoke different languages but it didn't matter. Understanding each others' words was not necessary to worship together. It was cool because the one word everyone knew was "Jesus." It was even more astounding to witness the success of this convergence when I learned that many of the nations had a history of feuding with each other.

The rest of my afternoon was spent with the church's pastor, who talked to me about an innovative pilot program where a new, self-sustaining community was being created. The community would be taught skills such as how to grow crops, make bricks for building shelters, or make crafts for exporting overseas. The leaders had the foresight to teach the people how to sell and also how to run basic accounting books.

The goal was basic economics: teach people how to generate enough revenue to support the community without having to rely on outside aid after the start-up period. If the people worked synergistically, then the pilot program should have a good chance of success. If successful, it was likely that the sponsors would get funding to expand the pilot to a second community.

I was impressed by what they were attempting to do in Lilongwe. There was potential for a significant impact on the quality of life, but more than that it gave the people hope. I prayed that Barnabas could get behind it with some financial support.

The entire trip was a blessing. Not only did I meet new people that I could interface with in the future, but I had gained new visions for projects that Barnabas Charities could support. I tried to be like a sponge during the trip and soak up as much information as possible to process later and translate into an action plan for Barnabas.

The people in Malawi are 14 million strong, yet they live a life where they truly do not have anything. I rarely saw children with shoes. It seemed like only 1 out of 50 children owned a pair. Most only have one set of clothes. They will go to a stream and wash what they were wearing, dry it and put it back on. Some of the clothes the children were wearing were so worn that there were more holes than solid cloth.

Similar to the traditional African pictures we see in the States, the women carry baskets on their heads filled with things like water and food. Depending on where they live, some have to walk over five kilometers a couple of times each day to get needed water. They are in desperate need of more wells.

Andrew took me to visit the only school in the immediate area. Seven hundred students came here each day; approximately 100 students are in each class. I learned that thousands of students would be there every day if all of the kids living in the area attended school. The reality is that most children have to work to earn money for their families, so going to school is not a priority.

The Primary School houses 1st Grade through 8th Grade. Some children walk 20 kilometers every day to and from school. If they want to attend High School, they must pay tuition that most cannot afford. They need the education to make a better life for themselves and their families, but financial and other challenges make it very difficult to do. And so the cycle of poverty continues.

Despite the difficult life these families lead, the faith of those in the church is amazing. The ones with faith in God are mostly the women and young children, who give us hope

The school building we visited in Malawi

for future generations. I won't forget one story told to me during my time in Malawi. A ten year old boy had accepted Jesus as his Savior after attending youth group for several months. Upon returning to his village, the chief and elders asked him what he was learning. The boy told them about the messages and the elders were curious so they told him to continue going to the youth group and report back each week to share what he learned to the whole village.

I admire the faith and courage of that little boy. This one child's efforts brought Jesus to the adults and leaders of his village.

Life expectancy in Malawi is only about 36 years. As a result, a staggering 60% of the population is under fifteen years old. Children take care of children. Abuse and oppression are seen every day. AIDS is thought to be the #1 killer in Malawi, but it's not; Malaria, which is preventable, is actually responsible for taking the most lives in this area.

With everything I've reported, you would think that the children are unhappy, but they are some of the happiest children I've ever met.

A school room in Malawi

After flying back to Cape Town and then driving the 20 minutes to Fish Hoek, I said my goodbyes to Pat Ball and to Pierre's family. I would miss them, but the three month trip was over and I needed to get back to my own family. Without a doubt, the people I met in South Africa made an indelible mark within me. I took the lessons learned in this trip back with me, along with dozens of dreams for the work that could be accomplished through Barnabas.

Children taking care of children

The Next Generation

Alex was jazzed and Torry was terrified when we walked out onto the bridge and looked over the side into the gorge. I had thrown down a challenge for my kids to bungee jump like their old dad had done a month earlier. Alex wanted to bungee jump as soon as he found out I did. Torry, on the other hand, didn't know if she was going to take the leap until the very last minute, but she faced her fear and did it.

To be honest, my heart was in my throat the entire time, but I did my best to play it cool. Watching your kids jump off a bridge, hearing them scream, and knowing exactly what they are feeling was truly frightening, but watching them made me proud, too.

Life is about taking risks. God does not want us to sit back in a comfort zone. He wants us to jump into unknown territories and realize that we can only succeed by His grace. Having a heart devoted to God is first, but having the courage to take a risk, especially when you're terrified, is a quality I'm proud to see both my kids possess.

My desire for my children to walk the talk as Christians is taught to all parents through scripture in Deuteronomy 6:5-7: *Love the Lord your God with all your heart and with all your soul and with all your strength. These commandments that I give you today are to be on your hearts. Impress them on your children. Talk about them when you sit at home and when you walk along the road, when you lie down and when you get up.*

Before leaving on the trip with my kids, I relocated to Florida so I could be close to them. I was able to live just a couple of blocks from their mother's home, so it was convenient for the kids to visit whenever they wanted. With everything I witnessed during my 90 days in Africa, it was important for me to expose Torry and Alex to some of these realities.

I wanted them to learn by being a part of something outside the sheltered experiences of their own lives. I was a teenager once, so I knew they sometimes saw the world with a tunnel vision. I had planned the trip to South Africa as an adventure with a lesson.

During our 2 1/2 week trip, Alex, Torry and I went on a safari, visited Table Rock, saw the directionally challenged penguins who made their home on the beach at Boulder Bay, and travelled to see the spectacular views at Cape Point located on the southeastern tip of Africa. We made memories and had a great time reconnecting as a family.

After the "tourist" stuff was out of the way, we also took a fact finding trip about potential new projects with a missionary from the area. Because of generous donations that had been waiting for me when I returned home from the previous trip, Barnabas had been able to fund projects and start making a difference right away. We brought a suitcase of medical equipment, money earmarked for other projects, and $10,000 for a man who lived in Lilongwe, Malawi, so he could go to Seminary School. Score one for God working through Barnabas Charities!

The trip with my children wouldn't be all work. But the kids did have their first exposure to the conditions people endure in a third world country. Torry was affected when she saw the housing and lack of basic necessities. It was espe-

Torry and Alex on a beach in South Africa

cially difficult for her to see the little children living in such a state of poverty. Her heart went out to them and she began interacting right away.

Afterwards, we had a brief respite enjoying a visit to Table Mountain, a well-known attraction because of the flat surface of the sandstone mountain that looks as if someone came by and sliced the top right off.

We left the city of Cape Town and the main continent behind us as we traveled along the sandstone peninsula that jutted out into the Atlantic Ocean. Cape Point is located on the southeastern tip of Africa among a huge outcropping of mountainous rock. The contrast between the rugged mountains and the graceful ocean was breathtaking.

We took a break for lunch at Cape Point and had our first of many encounters with baboons. Torry was laughing as she said, "There were so many animals you don't see in the United States. Baboons were everywhere! They were sitting on top of parked cars, chasing people who had food, and some were just people watching."

It was true that the baboons were funny to watch, but Pierre had warned us not to let our guard down around them because they were dangerous critters as well.

Leaving Cape Point, we travelled on to the beach at Boulder Bay where we saw a very peculiar and unexpected sight—hundreds of penguins! We knew penguins were supposed to be on the south end of the planet but it was hilarious to watch these directionally challenged birds.

Torry with a group of African school children.

For the next few days, we worked with children in several areas outside Cape Town. It was a little uncomfortable at first, even for Torry who was a natural with kids. As a young man of 17, Alex was a little more reserved. He wrote the following entry about his experiences in the Barnabas blog:

First, I would like to talk about the children we met at the Kids Club. About thirty kids were there and they were extremely clingy! They are little kids so they naturally migrate to anyone who will give them attention. It was hard to see that only about $3/4^{ths}$ of the kids had shoes on their feet and the rest were barefoot.

They didn't have much in the way of clothes either. We helped out for two days and both days a lot of the children wore the same clothes. It is just sad! We seem to take so much for granted in the United States. It really put into perspective how fortunate we are to be able to buy new shoes when we want them, when the children here only have one pair. And that's if they are lucky enough to have a pair at all.

The first place we visited was a township in South Africa called Khayalitsha. Most people live in tiny shacks and less than 1/4 of the people there have water or electricity. They gather odds and ends from anywhere they can find to build or add on to a shack for their families to sleep inside.

Our dad talked to a youth group today. He talked about faith and it was really cool to see him talking to a youth group like that. At the end of his talk, he gave them each a challenge (and us, too). He handed out R100, which is $13.00 U.S, but it's the average income for a week! The point was to show an example of faith with the money we were given. They could use it to help themselves or someone else. Next week our dad will ask everyone to share their experience and how they used the money.

We returned to the youth group of Masiphumelele Church a week later to talk about what they did with the 100 Rand. We found that the money was used in different ways, but every single person turned the money into a blessing of some sort. I didn't say whether they had to give the money away or use it for themselves, so it was interesting to see the results of the experiment.

Before leaving the previous week, the youth pastor, Sonwabo, took me aside to tell me that the money was given at a perfect time because his family was struggling to avoid having their electricity turned off. Then God touched Torry's and Alex's hearts to help by giving the $50 each had received as spending money from their grandmother to Sonwabo and his family. This amounted to an additional R700. Sonwabo was very emotional at the generous gift. It was by far the most money he had ever seen. The average monthly income was R500. So this was like getting more than a month's income all at one time, in addition to the R100 he received during the youth group.

A short time later, Sonwabo was working with young children when he saw a girl sitting alone and crying. He sat down on the floor next to her and gently asked why she was so sad. The girl reluctantly told him she didn't know where her mother was and that her father had just died. He looked at her for a moment and then offered to help find her mother.

They searched for four long hours before finding her. The mother was out of her mind with a combination of grief and panic about how she was going to take care of her family. She had left to take a few hours to pull herself together. Now that her husband was gone, the family had no source of income. Sonwabo spoke with the girl's mother for a long time and before leaving he blessed them with the entire R700. His kindness was a profound example for all of the youth, including Alex and Torry.

My children ended up combining their R100 to purchase pants, shirts, and shoes for some of the children. I was really proud to see they had giving hearts. I ended up giving my R100 to a young woman working at Kid's Club who was struggling to provide for her family. She never asked for the money, but I felt the now-familiar push to reach out and it was great to know I made her life a little easier that day.

It was interesting to learn that some of the children put the money in their Bibles for safe-keeping. Another child paid for food for a person who was travelling back to Malawi to live with his family because he was dying of AIDS. A young woman could not decide what to do until the day before we reconvened at youth group. She learned about a lady who had no money, electricity, or food so she went to the lady's home and gave her the R100. The two young women became fast friends and now visit each other regularly.

Many children used the money to help others, some took it as the blessing they had prayed for, and others used it for their own families. The majority of the people who spent the R100 used it for necessities like clothing, food and electricity. One young lady talked about how her family of five had only one blanket and they had to sleep together in order to stay warm on the cold nights. Astonishingly, she did not use the money for herself, but gave it to someone who she said had "nothing."

The blessings of the lesson had a butterfly effect on the community, confirming just how powerful kindness can be.

I saw the experience as confirmation that Alex and Torry were absorbing the lessons that I had hoped they would learn. They also gained a new appreciation and empathy for the people that I hoped would stay with them after we returned home. More than anything, I hoped the exposure of the trip brought my children a step closer to understanding that God provides all we need. This truth is shown through the Apostle Paul's testimony in Philippians 4:11-13 when he wrote:

> *Not that I was ever in need, for I have learned how to be content with whatever I have. I know how to live on almost nothing or with everything. I have learned the secret of living in every situation, whether it is with a full stomach or empty, with plenty or little. For I can do everything through Christ, who gives me strength.*

What a blessing it was to spend two weeks in Africa with my children. We learned, and laughed, prayed, and played together. I'm amazed at how God continues to lead me into more and more work and continues to bless me by allowing me to speak His words in my messages to the youth. The coolest part of all was seeing my children grow in their own walk with Christ.

A Man on a Mission

People say there is a difference in me when I'm working with mission teams compared to when I am at home in the States. I was trying to come to terms with this perception when I noticed that a few weeks after returning to the United States, I began to fall back into the trap of materialism. I didn't miss any of my American things and habits while in South Africa, but I realized how easily I could fall back into my former self. It was stressful because that was not the person I wanted to be.

The truth is that we all have, at one time or another prayed with one hand and sinned with the other. It's why God sent His only son so our sins could be forgiven. He knew we would continue to mess things up and succumb to our sinful nature. And Satan takes full advantage because he knows where we are the weakest and where to get a foothold. It's been said that the closer we get to God, the more Satan has to gain by separating us from Him.

I have come to think of Fish Hoek as a second home and I love working with Pierre and Pat Ball along with Extreme Response and Living Hope Ministries. I was excited when the opportunity arose to return to Africa only three short months after returning from the trip with Alex and Torry. This trip was going to be particularly special because the team was working with a ministry involved with HIV/AIDS awareness and support and our itinerary was jam packed! There were other opportunities for me to work with the youth group again, visit orphanages and we were going to team up with Living Hope to throw a special party for the people in Fish Hoek that were homeless.

One member of the team was an artist from Holland, Michigan named Lisa Schulist. She is a friend who generously offered encouragement and has given her time to work at several charity events. She's someone I can confide in and who will give me her perspective without holding back. Lisa shared how being invited to join the team impacted her life:

> Mission work made me want to become more involved in actively serving God. Africa was a great place to go for the adventure, but what really caught me off guard was that the people there are happy and clean; they have nothing by our standards but they don't envy. They have nothing, and yet they have so much faith. We pray when we need something, but all they have is faith and it's enough. I came to this country to serve and I ended up being the one to receive the gift. I think we could learn a lot from their example.

I was starting to feel more confident about speaking at churches and giving the devotions for the youth group, so when I was asked if I would be willing to give the Sunday message at Masiphumelele Church, my response was "Oh yeah!" The message I decided on was intended to motivate the congregation to move out of their comfort zone and bring others to Jesus. Taking a line from my favorite movie, *Braveheart,* the message was titled, "All men die, not all men live. What does living mean to you?" It turned out to be a good topic for the day because after the service, the congregation participated in an AIDS walk throughout the township as a celebration of life.

Prayer with the children

We made a great leap during this trip when Pierre agreed to align his organization—ATAIM (Africa to Asia Innovative Ministries)—with Barnabas Charities by taking on projects that could be supported by individuals or groups. Barnabas Charities would select projects, raise awareness and provide financial support, while ATAIM served as the constant feet on the ground in Africa. Pierre would travel to identify, document and evaluate potential projects since he has a good feel for what Barnabas can handle. Pierre explained to me that, "We are on God's time here and God only knows where we will be going and what we will see. He will move our hearts and show us which projects to select."

We agreed that many people have a desire to get involved in missions, but also feel that their contributions get lost in large scale ministries. We talked for hours to identify obstacles that kept people from sponsoring ministry projects. In the end, we decided to make it easier for people by sectioning projects into manageable pieces that accommodate varying budgets in a program called GO MAD (Go Make a Difference).

Right out of the gate, our first three projects were to grow the Mimi's Soup Kitchen ministry, Net Vir Pret, and God's Little Lighthouse.

Mimi's Soup Kitchen has remained fully sponsored by a family in Denver. Net Vir Pret, which means "Just for fun," is an after school youth program geared towards keeping children off the streets and safe from harm. This project and God's Little Lighthouse in Fish Hoek are sponsored by different groups of people who pool their collective resources. A number of people supported a playground project, a painting project and a project to repair a worn section of the school.

Others travelled from the United States to contribute with their sweat and hard work by doing the manual labor for projects that had funding but needed workers to complete the vision. I will never underestimate the power of love to achieve great things.

Just as things were picking up with Barnabas, In March 2009, I was called back to my home town in Michigan to run my dad's company, Medical Accessories Research Corporation (MARC). I had served on the Board of Directors of the company and recently suspected that something was amiss, but in my board capacity I didn't have the authority to look into what my gut was telling me.

I never intended to be a bean counter. In college I became an accountant because in the business world the accountants know where the money is; they have their finger on the financial pulse and are the first to know when the company is doing well or poorly. As a result of that philosophy, my first order of business was to inspect the books at MARC.

Unfortunately, I found a problem in the financials and after some pushing, the Controller admitted knowing about the situation. It was a problem for many reasons, but at the moment I was most concerned by the overstatement of our financial position. That's the element that our bank used to renew our line of credit.

For many companies, a bank will provide a working capital line of credit to help with payroll and other operating expenses. It is a safety-net companies use to meet expenses during brief periods of limited cash flow. Some months a company may access their line of credit whereas other months they may not even touch it or pay the loan back.

Medical Accessories was drawing on its line of credit month after month in a "borrow from Peter to pay Paul" strategy. The General Manager knew what was happening but would not confront the situation head on. It was pretty clear there were problems bigger than I originally suspected.

The company was known for its innovative product line and had consistent demand from customers. We designed and manufactured state of the art synthetic skin, sales displays, skeletal parts, and bones with faux marrow and blood. The company also specialized in cervical, thoracic, and lumbar spine models.

Our product line of artificial anatomical parts was designed for sales presentations, medical education, and surgical training. The surgical training arm was the fastest growing part of the business. We created patented simulated anatomical parts that replicated the look, feel and texture of the real thing eliminating the need of a cadaver. It was a cutting edge niche market, but the financial condition of the company had deteriorated to a point where there was no way we could keep the doors open for long without significant changes and capital from outside investors.

My dad has always been a brilliant visionary when it comes to creating companies and making money, but he was consistently challenged when it came to handling the books. As a result, his companies suffered financially even as their customer base and product line continued to expand. At MARC, the financial troubles were treated with band-aids of accumulating debt. It was a paradox: On one hand, the demand for our product was growing and the sales force was able to acquire new customers, but on the other hand the financial challenges of the company created a shortage of cash to buy supplies in order to keep up with demand so we could serve our customers.

During my tenure, I wanted to create the same philanthropic environment at MARC that we had had at GB Synergy, so I gathered the entire staff and let them know 10% of profits would go to support charities locally and around the world and gave our associates the opportunity to contribute. It didn't go over as well as I thought it would and some of the employees were pretty vocal about their opinions. There wasn't much I could do at that point but to explain that the program was entirely optional and stick to my guns about the company's contributions.

Gradually, the employees came around; over time the majority of our employees said they were proud that their organization contributed to making lives better and some even contributed their time or a portion of their own salaries.

There were times, I'll admit, that I wondered if I had made the right decision given our financial difficulties, so it gave me a great measure of comfort when associates started getting involved and excited about projects.

This process of decision-making in the business world reinforced in me the importance of following God's lead even when it doesn't make complete sense to me or others. I have to discipline myself to trust God. With each small step, I was becoming bold in my faith. "The Wall," as my employees affectionately referred to it, in my office was a declaration of my faith, a source of personal encouragement and a visual representation of my passion for South Africa. .

Black frames filled with photographs of children in Africa and South America filled an entire wall of my office. All different sizes of frames stood out in sharp contrast from the beige wall where they were hung. There wasn't a single person that stepped into my office who didn't ask about *The Wall.*

Life Is All about the Contrasts

How much more beautiful is a sunrise because of the night? Would we recognize happiness, if we had never met sadness? It's the paradox of contrasts; the differences make each more beautiful than they would have been without the other. This paradox was about to become crystal clear in my life once again. On one hand, Medical Accessories Research Corporation was surviving, while on the other hand new life was being breathed into Barnabas by a project everyone called, *"The Container."*

After a financially brutal first year in management, Medical Accessories closed 2009 not only in the black, but turned a profit. We did it again in 2010. However, the success we experienced in 2009 through the third quarter of 2010 was cut short when our main customer had major internal changes that resulted in significantly reduced orders, beginning in October 2010.

Our year long upsurge in sales couldn't be maintained without additional capital for expansion, but with the amount of debt MARC was carrying, no bank was willing to lend us additional money for operating expenses. Week to week, our challenge was to pay the employees and keep the doors open. In a meeting with stockholders and the Board of Directors, I candidly told them that there was a very real possibility of employees coming to work and finding the doors closed by the bank.

If it hadn't been my dad's company (and involved his retirement income), I would have cut my losses and sold. I also felt a personal responsibility to our loyal employees. This dynamic made the stakes very high and the pressure began to take its toll. I wasn't sleeping well and my body was requiring more insulin.

My internal conflict arose because selling Medical Accessories would mean that I could once again run Barnabas Charities full-time. I also felt some guilt for not being able to summon up passion about my role in business. It was complicated, but being separated from my work in South Africa and the contrast between a life of missions and a life of business showed me clearly where I was meant to be.

Pierre from South Africa listened to my story and wisely said, "If you sell the business, you also have to learn patience. God may not have the business sell when you want it to. It's going to be in God's time and that's going to require you to trust Him."

That was a hard pill to swallow. I struggled with giving it up to God throughout the entire painful process. The difference, the part that showed spiritual growth, was that this time I kept surrendering the situation to God and then letting go, whereas before I was just blindly battling my will against God's will. My experience is that when I fight against God's will I wind up thumping myself on the forehead with the heel of my hand thinking, "Geez, I did it again."

But not this time. This time I was praying hard and reaching out to different people for guidance and prayer. I can't say I wasn't still yo-yoing between letting go, then taking it back, letting go, then taking it back again; but I was fighting to let go now; not fighting to hold on. There's a world of difference between the two and God could work with my weakness. Our weakness + God's love = a win every single time!

In February of 2011, I had quite a few meetings with potential investors and what was interesting was that, despite our current financial condition, each one expressed an interest in buying the company. Since I had signed all of the notes in order to secure a line of credit, I was at great personal risk. I refused suggestions by some to declare bankruptcy because if the business failed with me as CEO it would be a black mark on Barnabas' financial credibility, not to mention the impact it would have on our employees. In the end, the only acceptable decision was to sell.

The interest in Medical Accessories was driven by the profit potential of the company. MARC needed capital to invest in research and development. There were groundbreaking projects in the development stage that large hospitals were interested in. Even without the new projects, the company had everything needed to achieve fantastic success in the international marketplace if it had a solid backing.

We thought we found the perfect company to purchase Medical Accessories in March, 2011. The man who was interested came from a very well-respected Christian family and was local to the area. He seemed to say all the right things but the negotiations were dragging out. Meanwhile, other companies had expressed interest, but we were up front with them about the deal currently underway. Our negotiations continued for what seemed like forever.

In July, both sides met with the understanding that we were going to finalize the numbers and the details of the sale. But during the meeting, it became obvious that the buyer was not a good fit. Again, I was praying that I made the right decision because there wasn't time for mistakes.

Not long after parting ways with the first buyer, I was introduced to another gentleman, also well known in the area as an established businessman with integrity and a straight-shooting management style. It was an incredible challenge to negotiate in good faith and keep all the interested parties happy. I had to deal with the purchaser and keep him positive about what the company could do in the future, while making sure he was willing to pay the necessary amount to keep the stockholders all happy.

Medical Accessories Research Corporation was basically a family-owned business and we were used to being successful. My father understandably believed the company to be worth more than what we could realistically sell it for under the current situation. In a meeting with my family I addressed the elephant in the room by saying, "Look, I understand that you will not be happy with whatever deal we end up with, but I promise you it will be better than what you will end up with if we don't sell."

I didn't know if it was God's will for the company to sell. I prayed over and over, knowing God was in charge and He would keep things rolling in the direction He wanted. My mom was my greatest supporter during that time. It was such a blessing to connect with her on that level. We met for lunch every week and she was my rock. She gave me strength by assuring me that I was doing the right thing.

At one point during the day it didn't look like we would close in time. I consciously thought about how my faith was weakening and I prayed. I asked God to take away the doubts as I surrendered my concerns and fears to him. Then it happened. We negotiated the final details from 7 a.m. until 4:30 p.m. on December 9, 2011 to complete the sale of the business. Everything fell into place and we all signed on the dotted line, collected the check and shook hands. Halleluiah, it was a done deal!

It was literally down to the last minute, too, because the bank called our note and froze our account at 5 p.m., the close of the business day. If we hadn't closed, the bank would have shut our doors the following Monday.

I believe Satan tries to interfere when someone has the opportunity to do really cool things for God. I think a lot of what happened was because it was going to be the first time I would be truly unencumbered and free to run Barnabas Charities full time. I made mistakes, but I kept coming back to God and I think that's what he wants from us. With the sale of the company, I knew He had it covered and for once I was faithful and everything worked out.

So, yes, I experienced spiritual warfare every day, but God was always present.

Roadblocks to Faith

In the 1930s a young traveler was exploring the French Alps. He came upon a vast stretch of barren land. It was desolate and forbidding, having been devastated during World War 1. Then, suddenly, the young traveler stopped in his tracks. In the middle of this vast wasteland was a bent-over old man. On his back was a sack of acorns and in his hand was a four foot length of iron pipe. The old man was using the iron pipe to punch holes in the ground. Then from the sack he would take an acorn and put it in the hole.

Later the old man told the traveler, "I have planted over 100,000 acorns. Perhaps only a tenth of them will grow". Twenty-five years later the now not-as-young traveler returned to the same desolate area. What he saw amazed him...he could not believe his eyes. The land was covered with a beautiful forest...birds were singing, animals were active, and wildflowers perfumed the air. The traveler stood there recalling the desolate area that once was; a beautiful oak forest stood there now...all because someone cared. [17]

During the same period of time that Medical Accessories was being sold, a project called "The Container" began with nothing more than an acorn of an idea. In August 2010, a woman named Barbara Watkins contacted me about a desire she had to send shoes to the children in Beaufort West, South Africa.

Barb first had the idea of collecting shoes after seeing pictures on the Barnabas blog of little children without shoes on their feet. In a third world country a person can die from a cut on the bottom of their foot if it becomes infected, because basic medical resources just don't exist in many areas. A child stepping on a sharp object when they live in a city dump is a very real threat.

I remember how passionate Barb was about creating this project and I offered to help however I could. In a way, being a part of this project helped me stay connected to my faith during the sale of the company because it was a constant reminder of the work I dreamed of doing. Being a part of something so pure helped keep things in perspective for me. Businesses are bought and sold, money is a fickle friend, but a child is a precious gift from God.

Barb started a chain reaction as she began to speak to others who joined in the effort. On one occasion she was preparing to kick off a new shoe drive and asked if I would speak at the Vacation Bible School where she would be presenting the challenge. I wasn't sure how much it would help, but I was fired up to meet the people involved on her team.

We met at the church, and I could see she was discouraged. I asked what was wrong and she told me that the cost of shipping boxes of shoes to South Africa was going to be incredibly expensive.

Barb had collected three boxes of shoes already and she expected that number to be as much as 10 times greater before it was time to send them. I was thinking out loud when I said, "You know...we could ship a container. That way, the cost per box of shoes goes way down."

We decided to check out the possibility. The word *container* can evoke many different images, but here we're talking about a huge steel container that could be seen aboard an ocean bound ship. At a size of 20 x 8 x 8 feet, a shipping container has almost 1,200 square feet of usable space. Barb told me later that she had no idea how I was going to pull this off, but I could see she was once again fired up.

I was like a barker at the fair, spreading the word about the container everywhere I went, which included the people at work. The next person to join the project was Michelle Weed, who said the idea of shipping shoes was becoming contagious. She told me:

> I got involved through work. My kids are 9 and 11 and they go to a small Christian school. The school does charity work, so I went to them and pitched the idea of doing a shoe drive for Barnabas Charities. They were jazzed about being involved and our shoe drive resulted in nearly 700 pairs of shoes from a school with only 137 students.
>
> Then, a friend heard what we were doing and she wanted to do the same thing at St. Mary's where her children went to school. They collected almost 500 pairs of shoes for the children in South Africa. What is really amazing was that St. Mary's School only had a little over 60 students!

Twelve hundred pairs of shoes from only two schools that had a combined total of less than 200 students. It was a shining example of what caring hearts can accomplish. The largest school Barb worked with was Allegan Public Schools, where one thousand pairs of shoes were collected! We also sent letters to the Crocs Shoe Company located in Denver who generously shipped us 200 pairs of brand new Crocs for the kids. The momentum was incredible, and the entire project started with one lady wanting to send a box of shoes over to South Africa. In the end, this effort collected more than 3,500 pairs of shoes for children in South Africa, beginning in August of 2010 through February 2011. Talk about growing a forest from one person planting acorns!

We had decided the container was the way to go and I was talking to Pierre about it one evening when he suggested we donate the container to a project in Beaufort West. It was a no-brainer. The container would be given to a project that serves the community. The project was being run without a building at that time, so the container would give them a home base and provide a safe place to store their supplies.

As the women wrapped up the shoe drives, I started to make plans for the actual shipping of the container to Beaufort West. I received a phone call from a group at a local church who heard through the grapevine about the container. It turned out that a member of their church named Bryan was moving to Lesotho, a landlocked country completely surrounded by South Africa, to become a missionary.

The church group asked if Bryan's personal belongings could be shipped in the container along with some boxes that were destined for an orphanage they sponsored. I felt strongly that it was God's will, so we agreed to let them ship their items in the container at no expense to the church or the missionary.

Then things started happening fast. We were shipping boxes of clothing and dozens of soccer balls in addition to the shoes, the missionary's belongings, and cargo for the orphanage. A completely unexpected blessing was the gift of new medical equipment from Airway Oxygen to be given away as well. The container of shoes had morphed into many different things for many people.

February 16, 2011 was the day we planned to load and ship the container. A few weeks earlier Barnabas had successfully purchased the container for $2,500 and all of the cargo had been delivered and staged at Medical Accessories. Everything was ready to be loaded up and shipped. So far, so good!

I tapped an old friend of mine to handle the logistics of getting the container to Zeeland, Michigan. It was delivered as promised, bright and early on February 16, 2011. We packed it full and the container left Medical Accessories the same day.

The plan was for it to go by truck to Chicago, then by train to New York, and then by ship to Cape Town. From there it was to be trucked to Beaufort West and the entire trip was to be concluded by the end of March, approximately 6 weeks later. If only it could have been that easy.

We ran into a roadblock when I received a phone call that the container made it to New York, but the officials wouldn't load it on the ship. The paperwork was not correct and the South African government would not approve the shipment into Cape Town. No problem, this was fixable.

I jumped on it and worked with others to get the paperwork approved. It took two weeks, but we finally received approval for the container to be loaded onto the ship.

Because of the delay I was informed that our cargo was going to be travelling by a different shipping company. As long as it got to Cape Town I didn't care what ship it sailed on. I fleetingly thought about asking for the route, but dismissed it, thinking, "How many different ways could there be

Loading the container in Zeeland, MI

to cross the Atlantic to get to South Africa?" I breathed a sigh of relief that the container was finally aboard the ship and headed to Cape Town.

Then another roadblock fell into place. The original shipping company was sailing directly to South Africa, which is a straight shot across the Atlantic Ocean, then southwest to Cape Town. The new shipping company went to Northern Africa and was making its way south from the eastern side of Africa. If I had known where the ship was it wouldn't have been a problem, but the ship had disappeared and no one had any idea where the ship was for three agonizingly long weeks.

I felt responsible for everything in that container and knew that several people were very upset about the delay, especially the church group who were shipping goods to the orphanage along with the missionary's personal belongings. The missionary, Bryan, was the most inconvenienced and ironically was never anything but supportive and encouraging about the container making its way to the destination. I was very grateful for his faith. I worked to get information every single day, calling every dead-end contact I was referred to. Through it all I prayed and asked everyone I knew to pray along with me.

After a few weeks of hearing nothing, the ship showed up at a port in Somalia. At this point I was thinking, 'What next, are the pirates going to take it?'" And I wasn't kidding. In 2011, the International Maritime Bureau reported on the very real danger from Pirates off the coast of Somalia, saying:

> It is the most dangerous stretch of water in the world. At any given time pirates are holding at least a dozen ships hostage. Out of fifty-three hijacked ships in 2011, forty-nine were successfully ransomed out of Somalia. What's worse is that Somalia doesn't take action against these pirates, nor can they register complaints from ships that are attacked, since it has a barely functioning government. A few years ago, there was no government at all. The area where most of pirates operate is about four times the size of Texas, so logistically it's difficult to ensure a safe passage for every ship in these waters. [18]

But the pirates didn't hijack 'our' ship or container. Shortly after locating the shipment, I learned it was back on a boat heading south. By this point, March had come and gone and we were looking at an arrival date of May 2011.

I flew to South Africa on May 30th after hearing the ship had made it to the South African port. The plan was for me to arrive on the same day that the container reached Cape Town. I was really pumped up about seeing for myself that the container had made it safely so we could deliver it to Beaufort West! I arrived, but the container did not. I called customs and was transferred from person, to person, to person, and it felt like I was walking in a revolving door, going around and around but getting nowhere.

I stayed with Pierre and his family during this trip. He could immediately see that things were not likely to be resolved right away and thought it would be best to keep me busy. He had a team in town at the time and invited me to travel with them to visit some new projects and then go to Beaufort West for a few days to learn about the projects that would be affected by the container.

It was a Godsend. Being with my friend Pierre meant that we would be praying and reading the Word which gave me the peace I craved during this stressful time. I had the privilege of meeting and speaking with the three ladies who were the intended recipients of the container and who ran the project in Beaufort West. In the course of that conversation, I realized for the first time that it wasn't the goods in the container that were most important, but the container itself.

One of the ladies told me she resigned her job eight months earlier so she could devote herself to working full time on the project that provided a school for the children and a variety of other community services. I was surprised that she would give up a job, so my curiosity got the best of me and I asked how she paid her bills. She just looked me in the eye and smiled as she said, "God told me to do this, so I quit my job eight months ago and have not gone hungry yet." This woman's faith is something I continually strive for in my own life.

The women who run the project in Beaufort West have a special place in Pierre's heart. He talked about them saying, "There are three particular ladies that live in this dangerous area but their passion is so great. They currently teach in the streets and their chalkboard is the hard ground. We plan to build an awning on the side of the container where the children can go to get out of the elements."

These courageous women exemplify the words found in Philippians 4:8-9 which says:

Finally, brothers and sisters, whatever is true, whatever is noble, whatever is right, whatever is pure, whatever is lovely, whatever is admirable—if anything is excellent or praiseworthy—think about such things. Whatever you have learned or received or heard from me, or seen in me—put it into practice. And the God of peace will be with you.

The ripple effect of the container project would bless many lives. I wondered if it was God's plan for me to come to South Africa at that time just to meet these ladies, learn about the work they were doing and realize that the real treasure was the container not all the stuff inside it. It was a moment where I felt that God lifted me over the wall to give me a glimpse of His plan. I realized that the shoe drive was somewhere down the line of dominos that had already started falling before Barb even initiated the phone call to me. I was thinking in such a narrow scope, but I could see clearly now that God's plan was greater than I would ever know.

Instead of being stressed out, I flew back home filled with excitement and faith. It was so cool, too, because I knew this project had started way before we got involved and we would never know how far it extended. It was awesome to know God included me in His plan!

After a couple more misfires, I received a call that the container had finally arrived and flew back out on a days notice, arriving on July 4, 2011. I was beyond excited and I couldn't wait to see the container. I was also pretty sure the missionary, Bryan, would be happy to finally get his personal belongings, not to mention the more than 100 boxes of goods for Beautiful Gate Orphanage. After arriving I went into Cape Town to see the container for myself. I just wanted to put my hand on it and know it was really there.

The next words out of my mouth were, "Umm... Where's my container?" Pierre was with me and we searched the Customs shipyard but couldn't locate our container. I thought, "No way, this can't be happening!" I was told that the paperwork was still wrong, so I dug in and spent most of the day on the phone having it redone, and then redone again. At one point, the customs employee told me that there was some suspicion that we might be part of a group from China who were sending items into South Africa illegally. It was utterly ridiculous.

Then I found out the truth behind all of the hassle we were getting: I was asked for money from a customs agent. Now we were getting down to brass tacks. I had heard stories about foreign customs agents soliciting bribes, but never believed it could happen to a small charity organization like ours. I told them the goods were not from China, they were donated goods from children in the United States, and I didn't have money to give them. We were told that we needed to leave for the day.

It was exhausting to remain calm and friendly when I was seething inside, but I knew it would backfire in a big way if I lost my temper. When I got back into the car, I just sat there for a minute in silence. The whole ordeal was so surreal. On the other hand, I knew it would work out because God didn't bring me this far to fail. That knowledge gave me the strength I wouldn't have had before.

There was a moment of good news on the second day when I returned to the Customs shipyard and got to see our container. What a beautiful sight it was! The moment was just as quickly squashed when I found that the container was empty. The entire cargo had been unloaded from the container and was being held in a warehouse where I was told it would be auctioned off in 90 days. I just barked out an incredulous laugh, then quickly regrouped and asked for an official that I could speak to for help. For the next two days I was shuffled like a deck of cards from one customs office to another. It finally dawned on me that I wasn't going to accomplish anything this way. I needed help, but didn't have any contacts in this country.

I'm pretty outgoing by nature and I stuck out like a sore thumb as an American businessman walking around in an South African shipyard. A man approached me after seeing that I was getting nowhere with the customs agents and I was happy to vent about what was happening. The man got on his phone and began relaying my story to someone on the other end and when he was finished, the man told me he worked for an importing company. He said his company could help and he was right. That importing company was fantastic!

They immediately took me to the warehouse where our cargo was being held. A representative from the man's company joined us and it was clear they knew how to navigate customs. He had a brief argument with the customs agent on duty, after which we were taken inside the warehouse and shown the pallets where all of our boxes were loaded. I let out a whoosh of breath that I hadn't realized I was holding and felt a moment of relief when I saw everything was there.

As before, the feeling of relief lasted for all of 10 seconds because the next thing they told me was that they were going to sell the shoes because their paperwork was still wrong. At this point I was arguing with the customs agent telling him they couldn't sell the shoes because they were donated and mostly "used" shoes! I told him with as much restraint as I could muster that the shoes were being donated to children in Beaufort West who were living in the city dump and didn't have a single pair of shoes to protect their feet!

Then everything changed.

I wasn't conscious that the customs agent stopped arguing with me as I pointed to one of the boxes and said "Open it. Look inside and you'll see I'm telling the truth!" So the customs agent cut open a box and pulled out a child-sized pair of shoes.

God arranged all of this because each pair of shoes in that box was in a separate Ziploc bag along with a handwritten note from the child who donated their shoes. Unbeknownst to me, the children from Corpus Christi Catholic School had written notes for each of the 500 pairs of shoes they donated. So, out of nearly 3,500 pairs of shoes the customs agent just happened to open one of the boxes with notes from the school children.

The customs agent read one of the notes that said, "Hi, I'm Emily from Corpus Christi School in the United States. I'm eight years old and I hope you can use my pair of shoes." That little note brought the customs agent to our side. It turned out that he had a soft spot in his heart for Beaufort West. God's hand was all over this project and I started to wonder what part the customs agent had in the grand plan.

We weren't out of the woods yet, because the paperwork was still incorrect and the goods weren't going to be released until everything was in order. If it wasn't resolved by the time they held their quarterly auction, the goods would still be sold. There was no negotiation about this. The customs agent wasn't standing in our way anymore, but neither was he giving any ground on the requirements.

Another two weeks passed as I worked with a friend in the United States, along with a local importer in Cape Town. Many other people never gave up hope and made phone calls to try and get the paperwork straightened out. At one point, I was actually told to give it up and go home because we were not going to get our cargo released in time. That was not an outcome I was willing to accept. These were just men and we had the Lord on our side.

That night I was at my wits end trying to figure out what my next step should be. I sent out an email to people who were part of this project and everyone else I could think of who would pray. I learned later that many of them sent my email to others, creating a chain reaction that resulted in prayers being sent up to Jesus asking for the container to be released from all over the United States as well as Australia,

South Africa, Ecuador, and possibly more countries that I don't know of.

That night I felt a sense of peace come over me and the stress melted away. God didn't need my help, but He needed me to recognize it. The fact that God would teach me this lesson shows how much He loves me. The next morning God started working out all the arrangements and sure enough, the container was released into my custody. I hired two helpers so we could get the container loaded up as quickly as possible. I just wanted to get out of there with the container before they changed their minds!

To my surprise, the customs agent told me that he loves what we were doing for Beaufort West and said to, "Keep up the good work." Because of the whole ordeal, we gained an ally in the customs office. Score another victory for God!

Arrangements were made to have the container transported on a truck to Beaufort West where Pierre and I would meet them. We left early the next morning and the weather couldn't have been more perfect. As we were driving, we received a call from one of the ladies who ran the project in Beaufort West to let us know the container had arrived safely and that half the town was waiting for us to arrive! It took from February 16, 2011 to July 19, 2011 to get the container to Beaufort West, South Africa from Zeeland, Michigan. I realized that night that this was another example of God saying, "Have faith, Todd; let me take care of the details."

When we arrived, there were so many people waiting that I felt a little uncomfortable about the attention—and I'm not a shy person. Among the crowd were the three wonderful women who would be receiving the container for their mission. After unloading all of the boxes and securing the room where the cargo was being stored, Pierre and I left to go to the site where the container would be set up.

It was my understanding that Barnabas Charities was responsible for paying the $1,500 needed to have the site prepared for the container, but when we arrived we were told that the municipality had prepared the site at no charge. God's grace continued to floor me when one of the ladies told me she received the phone call from the municipality on the same morning that the container was released. By the time we arrived, the container was already in its place. The first thing we saw were 15 excited little kids laying on the ground, trying to peek underneath the container.

Shoes from the container being chosen
by Beaufort West community members

Todd with the three women who received the container

We walked up and the three ladies who now owned the container were inside just smiling, crying, dancing, and praising God. We all celebrated and then prayed over the container. They said that they were throwing a huge event that night to celebrate and wanted us to attend. Unfortunately, I had to catch my flight home.

Psalm 20:6 tells us: *Now this I know: The LORD gives victory to His anointed. He answers him from his heavenly sanctuary with the victorious power of his right hand.*

Pastor C. Troy Sibley explained that in this passage, *"His anointed"* refers to us as believers. The anointed also refers to us being selected and marked by God to serve. The *"right hand"* is significant because it is the hand of approval and blessing. The Psalm is saying that because of God's approval and blessing, He has granted His children victory in the situations that they are facing.

Scripture held the promise long ago that I never needed to fear because the battle had already been won before I even began on this journey. It's a truth that my heart knows is true, but one that I sometimes can't wrap my mind around.

It would have been nothing for God to have the container sail right through in the time frame we initially expected. But that wasn't His plan. God patiently allowed roadblock after roadblock, after maddening roadblock in front of me the entire way through. Looking back I could see that God was putting me through the grinder because the day was fast approaching that I would sell the company and go into Barnabas full-time.

The container, repainted, serves as a center for the
Sunrise Community Organization.

Hindsight is illuminating because you can see God's hand in the story so clearly. He kept the container moving, but every step of the way was a lesson. Whether it was learning how to purchase a shipping container, learning the logistics of shipping to a third world country, how to navigate through the politics of a foreign government, to developing a relationship with a customs agent—everything served a purpose. And all God needed from me was faith to let go and let Him lead the way.

Ah yes, hindsight was no help at all while I was going through it, but I can learn from it and share my story with others. And that, after all, is the reason for this book.

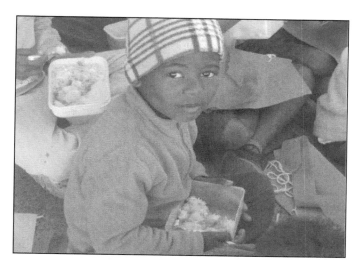

Child in Beaufort West,
happy with shoes and new hat

When Nothing Is Certain, Everything Is Possible

*Life is all about timing, The unreachable
becomes reachable, the unavailable becomes
available, the unattainable, attainable.
Have the patience. Wait it out.
It's all about timing.*

Stacey Charter

A ripple effect was beginning to be seen from the container project in Beaufort West. What started as a simple shoe drive was a catalyst for bringing Barnabas Charities into favor with the South African government. It was unclear how it happened, but Pierre received a call telling him they were being given 34 vacant greenhouses, a farm to grow crops, and another container was being donated to Beaufort West by the municipality. A house had been donated for teams to stay in and a local grocery store agreed to purchase all food items grown by the farm and greenhouses.

As mentors of mine, Jerry Carnill and Pierre Roux offered candid insights from a place of love about some of the challenges I would likely face in the transition from a businessman to the mission field. Jerry came into missions work from the business world just as I was doing and also has a gift of being a visionary who gets things done. No matter how far we come, there will always be plenty of room for growth, so it's with humility that I share their candid insights. Jerry started by saying:

One of the challenges Todd is going to face is that he sometimes tries to do Barnabas on his own, and that may be the biggest barrier at this point to doing all that God intends for him. He might not see it that way, but we all struggle with it. He has to get out of God's way and let Him do it.

The whole Gospel message is giving up ourselves and putting our lives in God's hands. The message is that you can't be 'good enough' to get into Heaven. You have to ask forgiveness in Jesus' name and then let God take care of it. You can't earn your way into Heaven. God wants us to turn from self and self-righteousness to His righteousness.

I think it's a human trait we all have, and something we are all working on; it's part of our journey. God made salvation so easy because He wants us to trust in Him. He knows we are going to make it difficult when it doesn't need to be. Everything is in God's time and in God's way. And God doesn't hesitate to shut us down to change our direction if He needs to.

Todd has always approached Barnabas from a "let's make it happen" business perspective. He may think that if he works harder, he's going to make more money; or if he works smarter, he's going to have greater success.

There's nothing wrong with that, but it's a business mindset. In mission work, things rarely happen in our timetable.

So when it comes to evaluating Todd, Pierre and I understand the challenges Todd is going to experience during this transition. In fact, one of my biggest struggles when I agreed to do Extreme Response full-time was that God was doing really, really well without me. I think part of the reason He called me was because we had full-time staff but not full-time leadership, and it became critical that we do so. Basically, my wife and I got tapped by God.

Pierre agreed with Jerry's insights into the 'culture shock' I would likely run up against and only had one thing to add. He said, "If Todd had his way he would save the entire world. Or, he will help Jesus do it…he has to learn to give up control to Christ."

I am not an extraordinary man. My life is an example of an everyday man who has gone through trials that many people have also faced. Sometimes it hurts, and sometimes it leaves an indelible mark on our hearts, but it makes us stronger, too. Through this journey, I have come miles in my walk with Jesus and although I still struggle to relinquish more control of my life to Christ at times, I will joyfully continue on my journey.

I've learned that what gets us into trouble and keeps us from achieving all God intends for us isn't all the *stuff* we have given up, it's that little bit we hold on to. It's like having enough faith to obey God if He tells you to take a row boat out into the middle of an ocean, but then refusing to hand over the oars! We, every single one of us, do the same thing at one time or another. So let go. And when you feel like your life is out of control and you grab on to those metaphorical oars again—let go again. Letting go is not a destination, it's a decision. An ongoing process that none of us will stop working on until the day we are welcomed into Heaven. Then, it's a sure bet we won't have any trouble saying, "Here you go, Father. I know you've got this." Faith is a tall, tall order and it's worth every terrifying moment to never stop letting go.

This is not **The End**

2008 Barnabas Mission Team

Barnabas Charities

In the Bible, Barnabas (called "The Encourager") sold his farm and travelled with the apostle Paul, spreading the word of God as a missionary. At Barnabas Charities we are passionate about our mission of FACILITATING GOD'S LOVE. As a non-profit organization, we strive to provide funding and support to targeted projects which enable them to be sustainable in meeting both their short and long term objectives.

Barnabas Empowers

Great hearts + faith = ACTION! Many people have the desire to reach out beyond their normal world to be a part of change, but don't know where to start or if their contribution will make a difference. Having targeted projects allows you to know where your money is being utilized – it's empowering to know you are a part of real change.

Barnabas Connects

Barnabas gives you the opportunity to GO MAD (Go Make a Difference) by connecting you with projects that you can support. You can do this as an individual or by creating a group that will make a difference collectively. You can choose a specific project or have our team designate your support to the most critical need.

Barnabas has Integrity

As stewards of Christ, our integrity must be unimpeachable. Through internal and external auditors, as well as annual reporting to all contributors, Barnabas Charities accounts for every single penny donated. The funds are then held in a Trust and allocated from there by a trustee to individual projects. 100% of money donated for projects go to that project. This level of accountability allows supporters to be bold in their faith, reach out and put faith into action.

Mission work is a team effort. It's all the people who are involved: the people who are praying, the people preparing things, people who are raising money or collecting goods. There is no one person who is doing a more important role than another person. It's a partnership.

How to Get Involved

Pray: Please pray for our vision and direction to follow God's will.

Organize: Bring together a group of friends, co-workers, your church, etc. and work with Barnabas Charities to sponsor/adopt a project.

Work for Barnabas Charities: We need people who can help find groups to sponsor projects and find funding sources. We are also looking for people who could serve as accountability directors out in the field where the projects are located.

Donate: Barnabas Charities is a registered 501C-3 tax exempt organization. Your donation is 100% tax deductible and 100% of the donation goes to the project specified. To donate, go to the website below and click on the donations tab or contact us by one of the below ways.

Barnabas Charities, Inc.
Fed ID #30-0215997
www.barnabascharities.org
www.facebook.com/barnabascharities
www.twitter.com/barnabascharity
Phone: 248-505-5554   E-mail: todd@barnabascharities.org

Todd, feeding an African elephant

What people say about Todd

"God is the one to do the life changing and Todd helps bring people to a place where their life can be changed; it's essentially facilitating God's love. He heard God's calling and was willing to jump out there and take a risk, putting it all on the line."

—Ron Cline, former President, HCJB Radio

"A leader… a helper…a friend. Todd Clevenger is the Santa Claus of the 21st century! His dedication and kindness to others has touched the hearts of many all around the world…thanks for being an inspiration to us all! Thanks for

touching our lives—you are our hero! God Bless you and the work you do."
— *Stacey Singer-Leshinsky, MS Ed, RPAC, Assistant Professor & Industry Professional, St. John's University, College of Pharmacy and Health Sciences*

"Todd is an ordinary guy, going through the same struggles as many Christians, who shows the love of Christ through his contagiously uplifting attitude. Through his work in Barnabas, Todd has helped children all over the world with their most basic needs: food, water, shelter."
—Eric McGough,,Managing Director, Northwestern Mutual Financial Network

"My ministry has changed because of Todd. We stand on the same principles and we sew faith into the lives of the leaders in Beaufort West, Cape Town and all throughout South Africa."
—Pierre Roux, President, ATAIM (Africa to Asia Innovative Ministries

"During my time at Masiphumelele Baptist Church as the Youth Pastor and Life Skills Educator at Living Hope, Todd was a guest speaker at one of our Youth Service meetings. I will never forget an American guy sitting in front of each and every one washing our feet as Jesus did to his disciples. Todd is indeed a servant of Christ, he loves all human kind irrespective of your background and skin colour."
— *Sonwabo Jacobs, Senior Pastor at Izenzo Baptist Church in Queenstown, Eastern Cape, South Africa.*

References and Resources

Scripture references are from the following sources:

New International Version of the Bible (NIV). Copyright © 1984 by Biblical Publishing, Colorado Springs, CO.

Holy Bible. New Living Translation (NLT). Copyright © 1996, 2004, 2007 by Tyndale House Foundation. Carol Stream, Illinois 60188. All rights reserved.

The Bible. New Life Version (NLV). Copyright © 2006 by Barbour Publishing, Inc. Uhrichsville, OH. All rights reserved.

BibleGateway.com. www.biblegateway.com. Retrieved November, December 2010; January 2012. © 1995-2010, The Zondervan Corporation. All Rights Reserved.

Cited References

[1] Brian Kurpis. "FAQS" HurricaneKatrinaRelief.com. 2005-2009 http://www.hurricanekatrinarelief.com

[2] C. Douglas Sterner. "Doug and Pam Sterner." www.homeofheros.com . Alexandria, VA Copyright ©1999-2011.

[3] United States Government Accountability Office (July 2006) Coast Guard: Observations on the Preparation, Response, and Recovery Missions Related to Hurricane Katrina. Retrieved 2006-08-27.

[4] Phillips, Kyra. "Bush Discusses Displaced Students; Department of Defense Briefs Press on Katrina Response (CNN Live Transcript). CNN. September 6, 2005. Retrieved 2006-08-27.

[5] ThinkExist.com Quotations. "Ruth Smeltzer quotes." ThinkExist.com Quotations On-line 1 Aug. 2011. 29 Sep. 2011 http://en.thinkexist.com/quotes/ruth_smeltzer.

[6] Staff writer. "If God is in Control, Why do we Pray?" Spiritual Journeys, Living Worship. www.intervarsity.org/studentsoul_June 1, 2011

[7] American Diabetes Association. Standards of medical care in diabetes--2011. DIABETES CARE. 2011 Jan;34 Suppl 1:S11-61. [PubMed]

[8] Slevin, Colleen. "Colorado hurricane volunteers say red tape is blocking their good intentions." Associated Press [New York, NY] September 12, 2005.

[9] ^ "South Africa". *Country reports on human rights practices : report submitted to the Committee on Foreign Affairs, U.S. House of Representatives and Committee on Foreign Relations, U.S. Senate by the Department of State in accordance with sections 116(d) and 502B(b) of the Foreign Assistance Act of 1961, as amended.* **1987.** United States Senate Committee on Foreign Relations. February 1987. pp. 282. Retrieved 2009-11-25.

[10] United Nations Department of Economic and Social Affairs • Population Division. Speeding Progress on the Millennium Development Goals. Homepage http://www.un.org/esa/population/publications/popfacts/popfacts_2010-1.pdf. [1], Census 2001 — Main Place "Khayelitsha"

[11] Saff, Grant (1998). *Changing Cape Town: urban dynamics, policy, and planning during the political transition in South Africa.* University Press of America. p. 85. ISBN 0-7618-1199-0.

[12] Minority Rights Group International, World Directory of Minorities and Indigenous Peoples – Zimbabwe: Overview, March 2009, available at: http://www.unhcr.org/refworld/docid/4954ce4123.html [accessed 22 January 2012].

[13] Zimbabwe". Trafficking in Persons Report 2008. U.S. Department of State (June 4, 2008).

[14] The Northern Rhodesia Journal_online: "Native Name of Victoria Falls," Vol. I, No. 6, p. 68 (1952). Accessed February 28, 2007.

[15] "Victoria Falls" Wikipedia, the Free Encyclopedia. Retrieved on January 22, 2012.
http://en.wikipedia.org/wiki/Victoria_Falls#References

[16] Southern Africa Places (2009). Victoria Falls. Retrieved on 2011-01-22 from Victoria Falls - South Africa Places

[17] Bible-Discussion.com. ©2000 - 2012, Jelsoft Enterprises Ltd. Website accessed 05:09 PM, August 27, 2012.

[18] Anouk Zijlma, About.com. "Somali Pirates, A Guide to Somalia's Modern Day Pirates" www.goafrica.about.com [accessed 31 January 2012].

Additional Resources

Diabetic retinopathy. American Optometric Association. http://www.aoa.org/diabetic-retinopathy.xml. Accessed September 27, 2011.

Warrick, Joby; Grunwald, Michael. "Investigators Link Levee Failures to Design Flaws." Washington Post. October 24, 2005. Retrieved on 2006-06-05.

Roig-Franzia, Manuel; Hsu, Spencer. "Many Evacuated, but Thousands Still Waiting." Washington Post. September 4, 2005.

Bruce Jones and David Callahan. "Leadership Talent Emerges During Hurricane Katrina Aviation Rescue Operations". United States Coast Guard. Retrieved 2010-04-14.

Nick Bonham. "Pueblo provides help in accommodating families displaced by Hurricane Katrina." *The Pueblo Chieftain Online* [Pueblo, Colorado] September 7, 2005.

Margie Wood. "Men of Action." *The Pueblo Chieftain Online* Pueblo, Colorado. September 12, 2005.

ThinkExist.com Quotations. "Stacey Charter quotes" Copyright © 2000 Stacey Charter. ThinkExist.com_Quotations on line 1 Dec. 2011. 30 Jan. 2012 http://en.thinkexist.com/quotes/stacey_charter/

"What a blessing it was to spend two weeks in Africa with my children. We learned, and laughed, prayed, and played together. I'm amazed at how God continues to lead me into more and more work and continues to bless me by allowing me to speak His words in my messages to the youth. The coolest part of all was seeing my children grow in their own walk with Christ."

-- Todd Clevenger

5237792R00111

Made in the USA
San Bernardino, CA
30 October 2013